PRAISE FOR
Mama Bear's Manifesto

"To experts in the fields of justice, development, and peacemaking, it has become clear that engaging and empowering women is one key to the transformation of families, communities, and countries. Recognizing that truth, Leslie Klipsch challenged herself to join the global sisterhood by raising awareness and funds for sisters in need. Now she challenges others—especially young mothers—to use their compassion and power to make the world a more just and loving place."

> —**Lynne Hybels,** Advocate for Global Engagement, Willow Creek Community Church, author of *Nice Girls Don't Change the World*

"*Mama Bear's Manifesto* is a ground-breaking resource for mothers. It is the voice of purpose for the lost woman surrounded by piles of laundry and weeping toddlers, for the grandmother whose home is a vacant nest, for the mama who's just put her last child in school and is staring bleakly at the long line of empty calendar days. This book reminds us that the very love which rocks our babies late into the night is the kind of love that can change the world. Leslie Klipsch not only provides the inspiration, but the know-how to begin to make a difference, right in your very own home. It is with great delight that I endorse this much-needed book."

> —**Emily T. Wierenga,** founder of The Lulu Tree and author of six books, including *Atlas Girl* and *Making It Home*

"The words of Leslie Klipsch contain helium. They're buoyant, lively, and wrapped in phrases that take your heart for a ride. They're also full of gravity. Every chapter is grounded, rooted in down-to-earth practicality, and revealing of a great truth—good parenting and thoughtful citizenship are serious endeavors that belong together. Klipsch pulls back the curtain of the perfect mom to disclose the meaningful life of an authentic mom. Reading her work makes me want to try parenting all over again, this time as a mother."

> —**Peter W. Marty,** author, speaker, pastor, publisher of *The Christian Century*

"Leslie Klipsch is documenting an important cultural phenomenon in our society. Over the last few years, I have witnessed a quiet, yet mighty force of millennial women who are transforming our traditional definition of motherhood. It is a movement of moms who choose not to 'keep-up-with-the-Jones.' Instead, they seek something much greater. They get on planes to volunteer in Africa, they organize fundraisers, and they blog about social justice. Across kitchen tables all over the country, women are taking action. Their sense of motherhood is not contained inside their homes, but expands to embrace our broken world. They are not dreamers. They are doers. The world is better because of them. *Mama Bear's Manifesto* will inspire thousands of women to join in transforming our world. Leslie has bravery, brains, and beauty and is leading by example. This is a movement that deserves to be told."

—**Becky Straw,** cofounder and CEO of The Adventure Project

"Modern moms are busy, tired people who want to help the world but often don't know where to start. *Mama Bear's Manifesto* is the book we need! Leslie's tone is warm, witty, and encouraging—just the thing to make us think *I can do this, too.* Her passion and energy shine through every word she writes, and she has just the kind of voice that I love to read. I can't wait to read more of her work!"

—**Claudia Chapman,** author of the memoir *Hypothetical Future Baby: An Unsentimental Adoption Memoir*

"Leslie Klipsch strongly believes that mothers, with their innate compulsion to protect the vulnerable, are in a unique position to change our world for the better. *Mama Bear's Manifesto* is an empowering call to action, and a comforting source of encouragement to moms in any stage of life."

—**Molly Sabourin,** author of *Close to Home: One Orthodox Mother's Quest for Patience, Peace, and Perseverance*

MAMA BEAR'S
manifesto

MAMA BEAR'S Manifesto

A MOMS' GROUP GUIDE TO CHANGING THE WORLD

LESLIE KLIPSCH

FOREWORD BY JODY LANDERS,
COFOUNDER OF THE ADVENTURE PROJECT

LEAFWOOD
PUBLISHERS
an imprint of Abilene Christian University Press

MAMA BEAR'S MANIFESTO
A Moms' Group Guide to Changing the World

L E A F W O O D
P U B L I S H E R S
an imprint of Abilene Christian University Press

Copyright © 2016 by Leslie Klipsch

ISBN 978-0-89112-378-1

Printed in the United States of America

Scripture quotations, unless otherwise noted, are from The Holy Bible, New International Version®, NIV®. Copyright © 1973, 1978, 1984, 2011 by Biblica, Inc.® Used by permission. All rights reserved worldwide.

Scripture quotations noted *The Message* taken from *The Message*. Copyright © 1993, 1994, 1995, 1996, 2000, 2001, 2002. Used by permission of NavPress Publishing Group.

Scriptures marked GNT are from the Good News Bible © 1994 published by the Bible Societies/HarperCollins Publishers Ltd UK, Good News Bible© American Bible Society 1966, 1971, 1976, 1992. Used with permission.

Scripture quotations marked NLT are taken from the Holy Bible, New Living Translation, copyright © 1996, 2004, 2015 by Tyndale House Foundation. Used by permission of Tyndale House Publishers Inc., Carol Stream, Illinois 60188. All rights reserved.

Scripture quotations marked ISV are taken from the Holy Bible: International Standard Version®. Copyright © 1996-forever by The ISV Foundation. ALL RIGHTS RESERVED INTERNATIONALLY. Used by permission.

Published in association with MacGregor Agency, Manzanita, Oregon.

Cover design by ThinkPen Design, LLC
Interior text design by Sandy Armstrong, Strong Design

Leafwood Publishers is an imprint of Abilene Christian University Press
ACU Box 29138
Abilene, Texas 79699

1-877-816-4455
www.leafwoodpublishers.com

16 17 18 19 20 21 22 / 7 6 5 4 3 2 1

Go forth and set the world on fire.

—St. Ignatius of Loyola

For my mom, Mary Barnum, the fiercest Mama Bear

And for Gram, Aunt Tess, Aunt Kathy, and Aunt Joan, who never stop teaching me the definition of LOVE in ACTION and showing me that it includes joy, loud laughter, and is often anchored by an incredible meal

Table of Contents

Foreword

Jody Landers, cofounder of The Adventure Project

M ost of us had kicked off our shoes and were sprawled in the barely lit hallway of the party venue. Women were calculating totals and scribbling on auction papers with tiny calculators from their purses. Others were hauling armfuls of gear and trash bags to the elevator and down to the alley. Still others were carefully collecting hundreds of used wine glasses, tenderly boxing them up so we could deliver them to the group of volunteers who were going to wash them. We had likely deployed every babysitter in town for the multitudes of kids represented by their moms in that hallway. With Leslie and sister-in-law Tesi at the helm that evening, we were wrapping up our annual Wine to Water party in Iowa. Through it we were continuing our efforts to raise money for clean water in Liberia.

Scott Harrison, founder of the nonprofit charity: water and former nightclub promoter in New York City, appeared in the hallway. He had been our guest for the weekend, and we had dragged him around to give his presentation about clean water to what seemed like every middle school and high school in eastern Iowa. We took him to churches and to Rotary meetings and to country club events. As he walked down the hall that night, he shook his head at all of us and turned his phone so I could see the text he had just sent his coworkers in the New York office. "These girls in Iowa have just put on a fundraising party that equals our best New York City events."

Those were fun days together with Leslie and our group of friends. Really fun. We spent so much time together. We laughed so much. We talked for hours. We dreamed together. We planned together. We worked hard. We stayed up late after our kids were in bed. We utilized naptime as the precious gold it was. We were discovering great joy. And we found a power to effect change because, as Leslie quotes in this book, "Our great joy had intersected with the world's deep hunger."

Community became our reward—a little group of mamas in pursuit of a great cause. And the coolest part . . . the very best part . . . is that clean, life-saving water still flows across the world for thousands and thousands of mothers and their families.

Leslie and I experienced this journey and growth process together. Looking back, we understand what a "magical" or "divine" season it was. All the lives of this company of friends look different now, but we all recognize that our time together altered each of our courses. And I, for one, am profoundly grateful for it.

Motherhood awakens something in us. It calls us to draw on resources we never knew we had. We suddenly have the power to do things we never thought we could. We have the ability to love our kids more deeply than we ever dreamed possible. And along the way something amazing happens. We begin to realize that we can harness and channel those same resources to bring kingdom change beyond our picket fences . . . beyond our own children.

Why? Because an intense and fierce Mama Bear kind of love—the kind that Leslie describes so well—will help you stay aware, stay connected, and stay in the fight for moms and children and all humanity, both in our neighborhoods and around the world.

Leslie beautifully dissects this process of the Mama Bear. She tells her story, our story, and the stories of many other world-changing moms and their friends. In it, you will find your story. In it, you will see your friends. And through it, you will begin to feel rising in you the protective and powerful roar of a Mama Bear.

On Becoming

Each friend represents a world in us,
a world possibly not born until they arrive,
and it is only by this meeting that a new world is born.
—Anaïs Nin

Some of my life's most profound moments and best memories have taken place on Tuesday mornings. Not, as one might assume, dressed up for dinner and drinks on a Saturday night, not pious and attentively perched in the church pew on Sunday morning, not standing and swaying at a concert, or attentive at an inspiring lecture or performance, and not even after work or class late on a Friday afternoon. There have been rainy Tuesday mornings, Tuesday mornings thick with the heat and humidity of a Midwestern summer, Tuesdays that were bitterly cold, and Tuesdays that were gorgeously sunny. The magic happened not because I was, for one glorious stretch, living in a young, hip neighborhood of Chicago and certainly not because I was blissed out by new motherhood. The magic of this rather typical midweek day happened because of the group that gathered Tuesday morning after Tuesday morning . . . the Church of Wrigleyville Moms' Group.

For years I was part of a group of young mothers who met weekly—children in tow—to explore the new terrain of parenthood with one another. Because the young church that we all attended was just beginning to establish itself, it did not have an ideal space of its own in which to meet, so we improvised. For a while we met in the church nursery (ideal for kids, not so comfortable for the moms sitting on the floor next to piles of plastic toys), sometimes in a pastor's office (more comfortable, but demanded a certain sacrifice on his part to surrender his work space with the very real possibility of discovering Goldfish or graham cracker crumbs on his desk upon return). We sometimes gathered at casual, kid-friendly restaurants, sometimes at neighborhood parks, sometimes in someone's small city apartment. Once we trekked downtown to the food court of the Merchandise Mart so we could have an hour of face time with one of the mothers who worked there. Lunch was followed, I should admit, by a pretty fantastic sample sale.

It didn't matter where we met. What mattered was that we were all searching for something. We were women who loved God and loved our children, and we found ourselves, as new mothers, in need of relationship. We craved community and did our best to establish a life-giving friendship with one another.

Eventually, the Church of Wrigleyville moms rented space at another city church, still in our neighborhood but with ideal accommodations—a large nursery where our children could play and build their own friendships while attended by sitters, and meeting rooms where we could get down to the business of discussing life and God and how God was presently moving in our lives.

On Tuesday mornings—no matter where we landed—we prayed, we discussed books and completed Bible studies, and we fawned over one another's children. As we got to know each other over the years, we formed what I believe everyone is capable of creating: a close community of invested individuals grounded by faith in God. Praying with one another and for one another transforms relationships. It takes you from playdate friends or bookclub friends to sisters in Christ. This bond, when deliberately cultivated, can turn into mature, beautiful friendships. For me, it was these very friendships and this small group of women that, in the long run, unlocked a part of myself I didn't realize existed. They walked with me through the dramatic ups and downs of new motherhood and helped me emerge with a previously undiscovered personal strength and a series of beautiful scars on a heart exposed by the intensity of a mother's love.

Motherhood, for many of us, comes as a bit of a shock. Nearly a decade ago, when I first became a mother, I quickly learned that no matter how many books I read and how ready I thought I was, I was grossly unprepared for parenthood. And though we all come to motherhood in different ways and with different states of mind, we all arrive at a place with a common reality: a living and breathing human that we're not always sure how best to care for and a form of ourselves that can be difficult to recognize. Personally, I shudder to think of what my early years of motherhood would have looked like had I not found the support of other women experiencing the same thoughts and challenges and joys at the same time.

My husband and I started out just fine. We moved to Chicago from our small Midwestern towns, we got married, and we spent hours sitting in bookstores, coffee shops, and restaurants. Jake and I were more than content. We were happy to sit around talking about education (we were both teachers and in graduate school), planning our future. We explored restaurants and museums with great frequency and pleasure. We spent late evenings drinking wine and reading books. Saturday mornings we slept in. We shared a simple, happy existence. We had a mental partnership and newly-wed passion. It lasted about a year and a half, and then everything changed. Nine months after our wedding day, Jake and I found out we were pregnant.

We met this development with great excitement. We couldn't wait to take the stroller to the neighborhood bookstores and restaurants, sharing the things we loved with a cute little babe. We assumed that ours would be the perfect coffee-shop baby, sleeping or cooing softly as we read and drank coffee. We immediately bought an armful of parenting books, started thinking about names, and began preparing our one-bedroom apartment for the new member of our young family.

Together, we made the decision that I would become a stay-at-home mom, giving up my career as a high school English teacher. Discouraged by the cost of childcare in the city and excited about the prospect of focusing on graduate school and more time with my babe, this seemed a sound plan. In fact, I looked forward to this new challenge and began to daydream about spending my days in our comfiest chair, a sleeping baby in one arm and a textbook filled with rhetorical theory in the other, a cup of coffee on the table next to me. I finished up at the high school where I taught, nine months pregnant and prepared for a new career of changing diapers and playing games.

It turns out that nothing prepared me for parenthood.

············· ♥ ·············

We brought our son Oliver home from the hospital at the beginning of summer and were shocked to find that we really weren't up for taking our new baby to the all-day, outside art festival. This, we took in stride. But then we realized that North Avenue beach is no place for a newborn. And then we found our son to be completely uncooperative in restaurants and coffee shops. We were thrilled with our beautiful little boy—100 percent healthy and absolutely adorable with his big eyes and huge feet. However, while we were counting our blessings and praising God for the gift of our son, we were also mourning what had once been our lives.

The transition to parenthood was more difficult than we had expected. Of course, we were sleep deprived. Of course, despite all the books we read, there was no instruction manual for our son. But in addition, I resented giving up my career more than I ever thought I would. Meanwhile, Jake found more peace at work than at home and kept longer and longer hours at his Teach for America job on Chicago's south side. I resented him all the more for simply having a life, getting dressed and going to work, while my life as an individual seemed over.

Worse, as the first of our group of friends to have a baby, we felt cut off from everyone we had known in our "former" lives. We withered without that once taken-for-granted support. I communicated my fear and frustration to Jake with rolled eyes and loud sighs, unwilling (or perhaps unable) to admit in words the full extent of my unhappiness.

What had happened? I had always considered myself a capable person, but it seemed to me that I was failing miserably at motherhood. I couldn't seem to find my joy. I couldn't find my footing. We were typically exhausted new parents and, faced with such a drastic lifestyle change, we were disenchanted and depressed. Everyone had been so excited for us during our pregnancy. No one told us we might feel this way.

Such things are difficult to admit. You've been given this gift—something that you have hoped for and planned for—and you can't help but feel ungrateful when you complain. We had trouble talking about these things, admitting our feelings. It took awhile for us to be honest with one another, to open up and confess that we weren't having the best time. It took awhile for us to ask God for help. For me, the latter took the form of a midnight conversation, locked in the bathroom in an effort to shield my husband and my newborn (who were both miraculously sleeping) from my weeping and my pleas. I literally cried out for some relief . . . some sleep, some insight, some clue as to how on earth to navigate this new terrain of parenthood. I had been a mom for three months and felt like I was failing miserably. Our families both lived in the next state over; I was overwhelmed and felt utterly alone in a big city. To me, it seemed as though a good night's sleep and any shred of normalcy would require some sort of miracle.

It was around this time that a woman I had been noticing for weeks approached me at church one Sunday morning about meeting during the week. I had been silently in awe of this woman—so put together and confident—for months as I watched her and her adorable little girl interact. Veronica and her husband lived in downtown Chicago in a high-rise building, and she embodied everything I dreamed about being a new mom in the city. She had a great city stroller, a no-nonsense parenting style, and a stylish diaper bag, and I had a hunch that she managed to take showers more often than I did. Her daughter, Kylie, was six months older than my son, Oliver, and their little family seemed to be thriving in ways that I could only imagine for my own. I sensed that there was much I could learn from her, as she seemed very confident. I jumped at the chance to spend time with her.

Veronica told me that she and another new mom named Sarah had been meeting for lunch with their children and wondered if I would like to join them in a more formal capacity. As it turned out, there was a group of new moms who were looking for community, and what our young church plant needed, we agreed, was some sort of moms' ministry. Because there were only a few of us who had children, it was up to us to pave the way.

On a beautiful Tuesday morning in the city, I pushed Oliver in the Snap-N-Go stroller down Southport Avenue to the neighborhood bagel shop and met a group of women who would become some of my closest friends. With each step I was incredibly hopeful, but I also held a bit of fear that I was about to expose myself as an inept mother. Because it was a group of churchgoers, I also felt insecure about my lack of biblical knowledge. How long would it take for people to figure how little I knew about God and the world? My life felt rather out of control and so did my worries. Motherhood had shocked me, and I was living in a period when I wasn't too sure about much.

Schlepping our strollers and diaper bags, six of us (along with our little plus ones) showed up at the inaugural meeting of our church moms' group. We took up a long table near the window and settled in with our snacks and our babes. And then we started talking. When I think back to the moment, I replay the scene with a joyful soundtrack. I see everyone smiling and I sigh with relief.

We spent the morning getting to know one another and sharing a bit about how we had come to this place and our journeys as Christians. We were a group of women who wanted to be intentional about spiritual growth. As excited as we were to discuss the pressing questions about mothering that constantly peppered our brains, we spent the first chunk of time exploring spirituality. God came first, then came best practices in parenting.

An important truth was revealed to me that morning: I wasn't alone. It turned out that none of us actually knew what we were doing. All of us loved God and our children and wanted to understand each of them better. Our table at Einstein Bagels was a tableau of C. S. Lewis's observation that "friendship is born at that moment when one person says to another: 'What! You too? I thought I was the only one.'"[1]

Something inside me shifted during that meeting and I found myself both humbled and emboldened. Over time, I began to shed the lining of pride and the facade of believing that I should have it all together. I didn't mind others seeing me fail. I appreciated their genuine concern and offers to help. What I got a peek of that morning was the highs and lows of women like myself. Hearing about their successes made me smile; hearing of their struggles stirred an impulse to offer help and prayer. These impulses have been persistent ever since.

What followed became a routine that we all came to cherish. For years, we were intentional about gathering on Tuesday mornings and engaging in some sort of study that would encourage us to grow as women and as mothers. We completed countless Bible studies over the years and read and discussed just as many books. We read about motherhood and womanhood and servanthood. We discussed prayer and fasting and discipleship and evangelism. We had vital conversations about our own unique experiences and the ways in which we felt God's presence in our lives. Our discussions were lively and heartfelt. We prayed with one another and for one another fervently and frequently.

The time spent studying and praying became the basis of our relationships. Our prayers invited God to meet with us and be present in our daily lives. We spoke freely about the ways in which God was showing up in our lives and the ways in which we were longing for God to take over. The women in my moms' group encouraged one another to read our Bibles and complete our studies, despite the busyness of life. By holding one another accountable, we grew in relationship with God. We thought about Jesus in new ways and through discussion saw the example he set and the words he spoke with new eyes. The trust that we eventually shared allowed our community of women to ask difficult questions and mull over new ideas. Rarely in my life had I experienced such intensely joyful and provocative study.

Wisely, we hired babysitters to care for our children so that we could meet undistracted. As our church moved from young singles to newly marrieds to new parents, more and more new moms joined the moms' group. Months turned into years and we continued to welcome new mothers and fall in love with one another. Tuesdays were meant for intentional study and conversation, but we also coordinated informal playdates throughout the week. Our children made friends with one another, and we relished the fact each of them had other "mothers" (or at least "aunties") who loved them.

With this positive influence in my life, I was able to find a better version of my new-mother self. My days started to take a fuller shape. I looked forward to Tuesdays and to subsequent playdates. I had the numbers of people programmed into my phone who had answers to my questions about teething and sleeping and the best place to spend a date night with an exhausted husband. I found people who would take care of Oliver in a pinch. I found women who were interested in meeting for coffee and talking about my interests du jour, topics that others in my life didn't find quite so fascinating or urgent. (Trust me when I say that nothing clears a room of twentysomething city dwellers like the topic of breast-feeding.)

As time passed, I felt less overwhelmed by being a mother and I began to enjoy it more. Oliver was a sweet baby who constantly amazed me with his curiosity and intensity. I loved watching him discover and holding him close to me. I was smitten with the little being that had changed my life so dramatically.

Jake, Oliver, and I moved to a bigger apartment in a more family-friendly neighborhood and hit our stride. We got off the couch to check out new parks and enjoy long walks with Oliver in the stroller. We discovered that almost every museum in the city has a great kids' exhibit and that there were some pretty great children's book sections sprinkled throughout the bookstores we enjoyed. Oliver, a very serious baby, started smiling at us more and seemed to genuinely enjoy living with us. Parenthood delivers a new lifestyle, one ripe with mistakes, but, slowly, Jake and I were able to get ahold of ourselves and discover the rich gifts of our new way of life. It would have taken a lot longer had I not found a group of intelligent, faithful women to learn from and create a community with. I had a new baby, new friendships, and a new desire to learn about and love the Lord. Within that first year of motherhood, a whole new world was born.

♥

The Church of Wrigleyville moms' group was a saving grace in my life. Grounded by our shared love of Jesus and bonded by our similar stage of life, we navigated the new terrain of motherhood with the help and support of one another. Studying Scripture and getting to know Jesus better propelled me and my mama friends to want to love others better and endeavor to see the goodness of the Lord in the land of the living, just as the psalmist proclaims.[2] We certainly didn't do this perfectly, but we did it with as much gusto as we could manage. We actively prayed for each other, for our children, and for our families. We held each other up in times of need and celebrated with one another on the good days.

Eventually, though, we began to take stock. We began to internalize what was taking place: how we cared for each other, supported one another, and shared God's love and peace with one another. Propelled by our love shown to one another and the love we sensed from God in our lives, we started to carefully consider some questions: Who else has need? What might we do to help? We began searching for ways to uncover injustice and use our relationships and our positions in life as a force for good in the world. Our group began taking on a new focus. Our conversations changed and we felt a nudge toward service. We took small steps and began packing care packages for college students during finals week; moms took their children to nursing homes to delight the residents. We were hungry to do good in our neighborhood, our city, and our world.

After three years of meeting every Tuesday, the inevitable happened. Second and third babies began arriving on the scene and small city apartments started to feel tight. Many of us, myself included, began to spread out around the country in search of more space and closer family ties. It was a season of tearful conversations and painful good-byes.

After a period of enormous consideration, Jake and I headed west with Oliver, who by then was a precocious three-year-old, and our little Elihu, who was just seven months. The good-byes were long and hard. But as sad as we were to leave the city, we felt it best for our family and looked forward to the new adventure that lay ahead. And though I mourned my Tuesday mornings and the friendships that I had left behind, God graciously directed me to another group of women who were actively answering the questions of *who* and *what* that I had just begun to ask.

Moving away from friends can be excruciatingly difficult. For me, Tuesday mornings after our move felt especially lonely. However, the pain lessened dramatically when my sister-in-law, Tesi, also a young mother living in our new community, took me under her wing and kindly introduced me to the women she had grown close to.[3] Tesi and her small group of women met formally on Sundays after their church service and then held playdates throughout the week. Their eyes were on Jesus and they prayed and studied with one another. In many ways, they reminded me of the group of women I had left behind in Chicago and missed terribly.

I soon began to see that this group also had an unmistakable drive to serve others and had several outreach projects under their belt. For example, after learning how children in dangerous domestic situations can sometimes be abruptly torn from their homes with little to no preparation, they provided hundreds of backpacks filled with overnight essentials (clean pajamas, a new toothbrush and toothpaste, a new stuffed toy) for their local department of child services. With the realization that kids in developing nations are so often hungry, they raised money to buy Plumpy'Nut, a peanut-based paste that helps treat severe acute malnutrition, to help kids with rumbling tummies across the world.

I was intrigued by these relationships and by the way they were channeling their friendships to do good in the world. They had harnessed the energy of their relationships and their passion, and they were beginning to use that power to do amazing things for others. For months, I watched my sister-in-law and her friends roll up their sleeves and share the love of Jesus. I listened to her heart brim with passion as her plans to raise money and spread love occupied many of our conversations. When you see such passion bubbling over right in front of you, it's hard not to want to be a part of it.

I was thrilled when Tesi asked me to take part in her group's effort to provide a fresh-water well for a village in Liberia that lacked clean water. It was just before Christmas and she and this group of women decided to persuade those within their sphere of influence to trade consumerism for compassion as they considered their holiday gift giving. The well that her group planned to help build turned into a grassroots campaign that sent ripples throughout our community. You'll read more about what this group of women accomplished in Chapter Eleven. To date, the Water for Christmas movement started by a group of stay-at-home moms in a tiny Midwestern river town has raised nearly half a million dollars and has provided clean water to thousands upon thousands of people. Just as my group of Wrigleyville mamas taught me to know, love, and serve God in powerful ways, so the Water for Christmas group gave me an outlet to continue the relationship.

The Water for Christmas group further convinced me that Jesus asks us to be movers and shakers and that a group of mothers just might be in the perfect position to fight injustice and love the world. This group echoed all of the questions that the Church of Wrigleyville moms' group had begun to ask and wasted no time in uncovering an actionable answer. In fact, their response was swift and ferocious.

Small groups can be a fantastic channel for carrying out the impulse of love and have always been a part of the church. Because small groups are thought to encourage relationships with others and to deepen our individual understanding of Christ, churchgoers are encouraged by pastors and other spiritual leaders to find community outside of the Sunday morning service. We can take our cue from the early church in which small groups of brave and passionate people gathered to learn more about the mysteries of a common God and to spread the love of Jesus. Since becoming a mother, I have learned the value of letting people into my life. Polite conversation is nice, but I believe we need the power of a group of people to unleash our strength and good intentions from the busyness of our daily lives, and help us overcome the apprehension we face at doing something big, and any lingering excuses. I've seen several glimpses of how cultivating *more* can be magnificently life-giving and ridiculously fun.

Maybe you've heard Margaret Mead's oft-quoted line: "Never doubt that a small group of thoughtful, committed citizens can change the world; indeed, it's the only thing that ever has." It is no coincidence that the subject she spoke of in this particular call to action is "a small group." By seeking out others with whom to share life and by gathering intentionally in a small group, we can establish a foundation for action. Of course, it's easy to gather into a small group those we find thoughtful and committed. It's no problem to show up with a Bible and a pencil. However, it's more difficult to jump to action. But one of the benefits of human relationships is that we grow confident in the people we are and secure in the love and kindness shown to us by others. We can use this confidence to buoy our response to the world's suffering. In other words, witnessing the love of God through other people can convince us of our own worthiness. Once convinced of our own worth and power, I have learned that we can use that power to affect positive change in the world around us in both big and small ways.

The women in my Church of Wrigleyville moms' group helped me deepen my faith in meaningful ways. Without them, I don't believe I would have gone on the journey of study and discovery, especially when struggling with the challenges of new motherhood. I wouldn't have gotten to know God the way that I did, and I wouldn't have taken so much stock in relationships and my purpose in the world. My sister-in-law and the small group of women who began the grassroots Water for Christmas movement took their relationships, their commitment to Christ, and their position in life and jumped to action. Together, they used the collective power that dwelled within a group of people and channeled it in outrageous, God-honoring ways to the benefit of the entire human family.

Attending the meetings of these everyday people, I witnessed a profound undercurrent of power and energy that we get from our relationships. I have been lucky to experience small groups of women who refuse to stress over the impressiveness of the snacks we bring to the table, but who are concerned instead about the momentum taken away. These groups of everyday, powerful women and mothers have channeled the energy of their relationships and embraced the possibility of change and growth and an impact on the world.

I was fortunate, both in Chicago and in my new home in Iowa, to be invited to help establish or join a group of mothers committed to growth. In both places, my heart was open and I was feeling just vulnerable enough to allow others to invite me in. I was humbled by new motherhood and later by being the new girl in town; however, during both periods, I was open to the call of God.

In countless ways, the world opens when tinies start calling us "mom." Not only do we discover the intensity and profundity of a wholly new love for another human being, but having and raising small humans can lead us to personal growth, new or deeper friendships and, as it did for me, a renewed curiosity about God. As the Tuesday morning meetings in Chicago—and later the gatherings in Iowa—began to pile up over the years, I experienced the value of and the power in a close and intentionally cultivated community. And I saw that with these relationships come great love and tremendous possibility. We are all capable of finding this groove and then grooming this joy, support, and purpose. As mothers, we are in a unique position to manage these relationships and cultivate a unique and meaningful response by engaging with one another and the world.

In writing the chapters that follow, my underlying desire has been to share the bits of wisdom that others have shared with me. I hope to guide and encourage groups of moms—whatever shape or form they may take—to use the stress and beauty of motherhood and friendship not only to support one another, but to work toward making the world a better place. When you gather together and pray for your children, families, community, and lives, God is present. When, bolstered by the love of Jesus and the love of each other, you serve others, your light—your vulnerable, sleep-deprived, ferocious, and beautiful mama-light—can't help but shine brilliantly on the world.

....

NOTES

[1] C. S. Lewis, *The Four Loves* (New York: Harcourt, Brace, 1960) 65.

[2] Psalm 27:13.

[3] If you find yourself in a similar situation in which you have moved to a new town and are looking for a place to get connected to other moms, try the local MOPS group or look for a city moms' blog or online group in your new region.

PART ONE

*If you see a mother with its cubs,
or with a smaller, younger grizzly bear,
the chances of an aggressive attack
increase exponentially.*

—Glacier National Park Travel Guide

CHAPTER ONE

Meeting Mama Bear

Anger is not bad. Anger can be a very positive thing;
the thing that moves us beyond the acceptance of evil.

—Sister Joan Chittister

Be honest. We've all been there.

You're at the park, watching your sweet child play. You're enjoying your coffee, daydreaming about naptime, or thinking about dinner. And then you glance your son's or daughter's way and you see it—a classic moment of childhood injustice.

It might look like this: there's a group of three or four children playing together in their exclusive circle. They're laughing, talking, maybe pushing trucks in the sand. Your child, your precious child, is naturally curious. He wants to push trucks with this group of happy children. He wants to be a part of the circle. He approaches cautiously, words are exchanged, and then he turns away dejected. You know all too well what has happened.

Your child finds you on the playground and is heartbroken. The kids won't include him in the game; they won't let him play. You are as shocked as he is. You can't quite understand how this could have happened to your precious boy.

How could they not see the specialness of your child? He exudes special.

Your child is hurting. So are you.

After all, it's your heart and it's outside of your body.[1]

There are all sorts of reactions to this challenge. Some parents may offer their child a hug and a juice box. Perhaps there is a short lecture about kindness and how we might have handled the situation differently if we were the ones inside the circle. Some might choose to ignore the group and the hurt and simply tell their child to find another toy or game or piece of park equipment, assuring him that he can do better than those small-minded peers. Some might approach the group of children and give them a piece of their mind. Regardless of how you decide to handle the situation, there is an unmistakable feeling rumbling under the surface: anger.

In this case, the anger that boils under our skin is over a classic juvenile rejection. Our child's feelings are hurt and we feel it in our guts and our hearts. We ache for our children as they grow up in a sometimes cold and hurtful world. The cut is deep and the wound raw. We realize in such moments that though the umbilical cord has been cut, we are still intimately connected.

Because of the universal nature of this intense feeling of protection and anger for our offspring, it has a name: the Mama Bear. This is a moniker familiar to all of us because, in our current culture, the comparison is often made between human mothers and mama bears. Often, in conversation with our peers, we'll hear a tale of hurt and injustice followed by the statement: "My Mama Bear came out."

At this we take a step back. We hear the phrase and we know she means business.

In the wild, if something comes between a bear and her cub, the mother will attack and do anything necessary to protect her young. She comes out roaring and no one doubts her intensity. Female bears are defensive of their young and have been known to viciously attack at the first glimpse of a threat. Just imagine a three-hundred-pound mass of anger seeking vengeance. This is not a passive scene.

On the playground, we know that even the most even-tempered, well-mannered mother, regardless of size or stature, possesses this ferocity inside. If pressed, Mama Bear will come out swinging and swiping. She will show her claws. You mess with my babies, as they say, and you'll meet my Mama Bear.

Perhaps you're acquainted with the power of your own Mama Bear. I am the mother of three young children and with great certainty I sense a Mama Bear lurking inside me. But, as a lover of peace and a classic avoider of conflict, I have to admit that Mama Bear makes me nervous, and I shudder a bit when I think of her being roused. I have experienced rage over comments that people have made about my children. I have witnessed moments of dejection and rejection and have been incensed. I have definitely met my Mama Bear, but I'm not quite convinced that I've unleashed her full power or explored her enormous capacity.

Mama Bear's passion is unique and ripe with potential. Though I cannot advocate for Mama Bear in all situations or champion her more petty grievances, I would like to harness her power and set her loose to exhibit some measured fury and intimidation in the right situation. What if we could somehow take the rage of Mama Bear and unleash her power when we read about injustice or hear stories that break our hearts? What if Mama Bear would strike just as quickly and hotly when she learned of an inequality half a world away as she might at the neighborhood playground? What if she could exist in this world with a perspective larger than her own?

What if we could begin to take on the struggles of others with the same intensity as we attack our own?

With this in mind, I have begun to try to capture the instinct of my Mama Bear swinging her arms, trying to free herself from the captivity of my body. I want to remember the rumble and the rage and I want to channel it for good. "Hope has two beautiful daughters," goes a statement widely attributed to Augustine of Hippo, the influential North African saint. "Their names are anger and courage. Anger that things are the way they are. Courage to make them the way they ought to be."[2]

If we could allow Mama Bear to show her teeth not just when our own child is hurting but when we see another human being suffer, I am convinced that we, as mothers, could wreak havoc on injustice and summon radical, forceful, lumbering change. We could be the protectors of not just our own offspring, but of the baby bears all over the world. "Find somebody who is depressed, tired, exhausted; you get them angry and it's like rocket fuel. I mean . . . it is unbelievable energy and stimulus. There is power within us when we're angry that can frighten us," says writer and pastor Rob Bell in his short film "Store."[3]

I think we all know this to be true. I, for one, have spent plenty of time on the phone passionately recounting the things that have angered me throughout the day. Venting to my friends, my partner, or my own mother offers momentary solace, but when I'm really angered I often find myself simmering without comfort in sight. I have been moved to punch pillows, slam doors, throw tissue boxes across the room, stamp my feet, and raise my voice. None of these things have been terribly productive (or perhaps even very mature), but they all hint to me that I am capable of *wild* emotion. I've felt it. And I believe these moments come as opportunities not to tame, but to train.

When we find ourselves simmering and approaching our boiling point, grab the stirring and memorize it. Then, pull it back out for a moment that matters.

Often, the times that I feel the heat in my cheeks are over things that I would laugh about if I really stopped to think. So what if another mother offers unsolicited advice about my parenting choices? Why worry about my six-year-old's playing time on the Little League field? Of course we don't want to trivialize the very real feelings of the everyday challenges that we face, but in the grand scheme of things, the problems that I tend to get bent out of shape about are typically fairly meaningless.

I'll be honest. I've found that identifying the moment of when to listen to my pure Mama Bear emotion can be as difficult as convincing my tired toddler that she does in fact need to wear shoes strolling the aisles of the grocery store. It takes persuasion and persistence. It takes creativity. And sometimes it requires the conventional parenting wisdom of choosing your battles.

As mothers, we need to take our own advice and calmly talk ourselves into entering the appropriate battles. We make thousands of decisions every single day; we offer choices and we make concessions. We know the practice well. Maybe we can persuade ourselves to choose and channel our anger wisely and train ourselves to become incensed about things that are bigger than the kids at the park or the coach of your child's soccer team.

Mama Bear must choose her battles.

There are times when our children need their mother to stand up for them. During these moments, Mama Bear *should* and *will* emerge. We need to advocate in our child's best interest, and sometimes Mama Bear needs to give us a push to do so. But chances are, at the end of the day, she'll have something left over. She has powerful reserves and can become not just a voice for her own offspring, but for others as well. Mama Bear can strengthen the voices of those who go unheard. She can help find their rumble and encourage a growl. Without our guidance, Mama Bear's strength is squandered. Her outrage is wasted. She seems selfish and stumbling, when really, she has a heart for justice and the courage to charge.

What if your Mama Bear got worked up about the young girls being kept from school in Pakistan? What if she noticed that baby bears in her very own school district don't have winter coats when the snow begins to fall? What if she heard about the mothers in Ethiopia who must take to the streets to beg for a single cup of milk for their languishing toddlers? What if she allowed the images of Syrian refugees with no certain future to resonate in her heart? What if the gun violence on our city streets and in our suburban schools shook her to action? These are the things that warrant rage and anger. These are the issues that deserve a Mama Bear to come out swinging and swiping and fighting for justice. In the human family, we need Mama Bear to advocate for and protect the young.

Mothers are uniquely built to do this. There is gentleness in the way that we rock our babies. There is great delicacy in the way we kiss our children good-night. But a mother's love, as beautiful and tender as it might be, should not be underestimated. Remember that behind every endearing moment shared between mother and child, Mama Bear is lurking. Mothers are capable of extraordinary care, and it is not limited to the way we love our own offspring. Our care and power can transcend our own homes and families and towns.

The short film "Store" ends with words that call the viewer to action. "May you become aware of your anger. May you learn to channel it, to focus it, to direct it into something beautiful. And may it fuel sacred acts of healing and restoration."[4] Because mothers have a unique perspective and a secret weapon lurking inside, and because of the inarguable power of an individual who makes the decision to shine love into the places that are dark and broken, I am convinced that mothers who are aware of the larger world and who are ready to act will become a force of tremendous change and a conduit of absolute love in action.

Mamas, let's identify what makes us angry and take note of the moments and of the stories that stir our souls and sting our eyes. Let's ask Mama Bear how she would react. And then let's watch her powerful, sharp claws point to the sky in an act of solid intimidation. Let's invite her to open her mouth and show the world her gritting teeth. Let's let her hair stand on end.

And then, let's take that impulse—the unmistakable power and passion—and use it as the fuel for something absolutely beautiful and for something undeniably good.

NOTES

[1]"Making the decision to have a child—it is momentous. It is to decide forever to have your heart go walking around outside your body." Elizabeth Stone, author of *A Boy I Once Knew*, wrote this. I first read it in a card given to me by my mother's friend at a baby shower celebrating the arrival of my firstborn. To me, it perfectly describes the intensity, physicality, and visceral nature of motherhood.

[2]Attributed to Augustine of Hippo.

[3]Rob Bell, quote from video "Store," *NOOMA* 016 (Flannel, 2007), https://flannel.org/products/nooma-store-016. *NOOMA* (www.nooma.com) is a series of twenty-four short films that presents an idea, challenges thinking, and prompts discussion among viewers. These short films could be a great basis for a women's study group.

[4]Ibid.

CHAPTER TWO

Identifying the Rumble

Take these shoes, click-clacking down some dead-end street.
Take these shoes and make them clean. Take this soul, stranded
in some skin and bones. Take this soul and make it sing.

—U2, "How to Dismantle the Atomic Bomb"

I dentifying what makes our Mama Bear rumble is most effectively a community endeavor. What makes me angry is quite different than what makes my sister bristle or my best friend turn red with rage. We trade stories and fears and often end up educating one another in the process. How many great conversations have begun with phrases like, "You'll never guess what I read today," or "Did you hear that segment on the radio about . . ."? Throw in a glass of wine and some spinach-artichoke dip, and you have the makings of a wonderful evening.

The fruit of great conversation does, however, require that we have our eyes wide open and are awake to the world around us. Often, I am tempted to ignore the news, finding it too depressing to take in. "Can't we talk about something less intense?" I might whine occasionally. Of course, there is a time and place for everything, even the current-events conversation du jour. And though I do not offer an around-the-clock invitation to the pundits, as a citizen of the world, I have a responsibility to be awake to both the beauty and the struggle around me, so I keep a newspaper on the homepage of my computer, and I listen to the news when I'm in the car. As theologian Karl Barth advised the young scholars of his time: take the Bible in one hand, the newspaper in the other, and read them both.

Being awake to the world allows us to be more fully alive in it. It expands our minds and trains our hearts to new levels of compassion. A friend of mine inspired me to write these words on a notecard and hang it up in my kitchen so that I am sure to notice it every day: "Lord, keep me from harm, from ignorance, and from heartlessness." It is an intention that requires me to open up my heart to my surroundings and to the world around me, even though truths are sometimes unpleasant. In addition to the overwhelming beauty and good of humanity, there is undeniable darkness in the world. It is up to us as unique individuals to shine our lights on the injustice that we see—the injustice that resonates with us and elicits a feeling of anger, the injustice that ignites our Mama Bear. We open our hearts and shine our lights and then tell our friends. We share links. We pour another cup of coffee. We ban phones from the dinner table and look each other in the eye. We walk side by side pushing strollers to the park. We take turns telling our stories, listening, and growing.

This sharing of news and experiencing the world together—this is part of our design. Within our small communities, families, and circles of friends, we learn from one another's views and passions. There is great beauty in the suggestion that we are all part of one big body of witnesses. As Paul writes in Corinthians, we are the hands and the feet, the head and the shoulders of Christ. We all make up different parts of one body in Christ. A group of moms is a microcosm of this idea. Just as popular culture loves to assign roles and personalities to the stroller-pushing, coffee-drinking, stay-at-home mommy set (the yoga mom, the soccer mom, the minivan-driving mom), perhaps we can realize the unique facets of each of our diverse personalities, filled with nuance and beauty, and then use them for a community mission. We can direct our conversations and learn from one another.

When we meet together within a community of moms to discuss the happenings of our daily lives, we will hopefully stretch our conversation to the larger issues present in our neighborhood, city, and world. It can be refreshing when a conversation turns from a session of venting into a session of solutions. As we discipline ourselves to foster this type of discourse, we create healthy, fulfilling, honorable relationships.

As humans, we find it easier and more enjoyable to embrace gossip. But why waste our time talking about other *people* when we can gather with intelligent minds to talk about *ideas*? Though this can be difficult, banishing the desire to linger in shallow conversation is imperative to the health of our relationships. Personal discipline and integrity are an important part of healthy adult friendships and the benefits of fostering them within your relationships are tenfold. Writer and activist Lynne Hybels puts it this way in her book *Nice Girls Don't Change the World*: "Being a good woman means trading the safe, passive, people-pleasing behavior of niceness for the dynamic power of true goodness. It means moving from the weakness and immaturity of girlhood toward the strength and maturity of womanhood."[1] We can bring our best selves to our relationships and work hard to bring integrity and energy to our conversations.

After I gave birth to our first child, Mama Bear began to rumble inside me. As I mentioned in the introduction to this book, this occurred around the same time that I joined the moms' group that ultimately made a life-changing impact on the way I exist in this world. During our precious hour of time to ourselves, we pointedly discussed the books we were reading or the studies that we were completing, and we worked hard to intentionally center our conversations. We prayed for and learned from one another. We were careful not to talk about the sleep habits of our children or the best stroller on the market. We talked about these things, too, but not until lunch after our meeting, or at the park later in the week. The hour that we spent one morning each week was sacred time, and we honored our purpose: to grow in friendship and to better know, love, and serve our God. This group of women became a safe place to get to know our new-mama selves and sort out all the power that new motherhood held.

It was during these conversations centering on books and larger questions that I learned what made other people most happy, what caused them the most sadness, and what made their blood boil. I learned that my friend Holly's heart burned for justice and that Jen had endless energy for anyone she sensed was suffering in ways big or small. I discovered that Tasha was sensitive to issues of physical suffering and that Kara longed to use her gift with numbers in a fruitful way. Our conversations were real and revealing, and I believe the structure of our time together had something to do with that.

These women encouraged me to open my eyes to the world— just knowing them and the scope of things they were passionate about made me a more compassionate person. Together we reached for God's rumble and prayed that it would resonate within us. Because we structured our time each week, our relationships had an added depth. The conversations were revealing. I could see the things that stirred the Mama Bear within each of my girlfriends, and I respected the power they held within.

Our individual actions matter. God gives us opportunities at every turn to love those around us in both big and small ways. Holding the door for someone at a coffee shop, shoveling the neighbor's walk, giving someone an unexpected and heartfelt compliment—all of these are simple acts of individual kindness that can make the world a sweeter place. A single person can accomplish these little things each and every day, and their impact just might propel the recipient of the small act of grace to understand God a bit better or to love someone else in a similar way.

As individuals, we have the power to refuse to buy products from companies that do not treat their workers humanely. We have the power to avoid places or organizations that discriminate. Our little voices can have a big impact. We must never underestimate the power of one. However, once we understand and believe in the power that each of us possesses within, we can grow it in exponential ways. If each of us holds within us an individual strength, consider the impact that a group of people—each person with their own unique talents and circle of influence—can have on God's kingdom here on earth. There is no shortage of need—it is all around us. Every community, big or small, will benefit from acts of kindness intended to relieve a bit of pain, summon a smile, or change a life forever.

"Above all, love each other deeply," writes Peter. "Offer hospitality to one another without grumbling. Each of you should use whatever gift you have received to serve others, as faithful stewards of God's grace in its various forms" (1 Pet. 4:8–10). Consider the rumble if a group of riled-up Mama Bears gathered together for a common need. Imagine the impact they might have on the lives of those around them. Think of the good they might do.

What if your mom posse made an exaggerated effort to, week after week, gather for a purpose larger than yourselves? What if your group of friends was to take the foundation you've established and start to consider the possibilities of life-changing work?

Maybe your group is already doing this. Maybe you could do more.

I can't help but dream about what a church community might look like if a moms' group took the reins and started acting. What would it look like if a group of women with a Mama Bear waiting under the surface, with all of their intensity and all of their gifts, took it upon themselves to spread their compassion and their wealth and their talent with the ferocity of a mother's love? How might a neighborhood become better or safer? How might a community benefit? How might the world be changed?

> New prophets are rising up who try to change the future, not just predict it. There is a movement bubbling up that goes beyond cynicism and celebrates a new way of living, a generation that stops complaining about the church it sees and becomes the church it dreams of. And this little revolution is irresistible. It is a contagious revolution that dances, laughs, and loves.[2]

This is what Shane Claiborne, the writer and activist behind the book *The Irresistible Revolution*, tells us. New prophets? Mama Bears? Hope for a new tomorrow—a tomorrow where not only our own flesh and blood might be bathed in love and showered in grace, but those down the street or half a world away might experience it as well.

In no way is it a stretch of the imagination to envision a group of mothers making a radical difference to those around them. In fact, it may not even be seen as radical; it's what mothers do. Mothers thrive in the trenches. Our work is dirty and often thankless. We can't help it—if there is a job that needs to be done, a mother is often the one to jump to action. Never underestimate a group of mothers who listen to the call of a task needing to be completed. Once you realize this—once you start to believe that you could be part of an irresistible revolution and you start discussing it with your mama friends—this is when the love and laughter, purpose and fun, will begin.

We bring to motherhood an abundant amount of passion, personal interests, and unique talents. Motherhood, in turn, awakens a fierce love in our hearts. Mama Bear takes root. Hopefully, we have our eyes open to the larger world and allow some anger to boil underneath the surface of our gentle mama facade. Put together, this combination is one of tremendous power and beauty, just waiting to be tapped, just waiting to unfold.

Author and activist Lynne Hybels reinterprets Margaret Mead's oft-quoted words, "Never doubt that a small group of thoughtful, committed citizens can change the world." Hybels's version is this: "Never doubt that a community of thoughtful, committed women, filled with the power and love of God, using gifts they have developed, and pursuing passions planted in them by God—never doubt that these women can change the world."[3]

Have you begun to feel your Mama Bear lurking inside of you? Have you ever witnessed a friend brim with passion or anger? Ladies, it's time to take it and channel it. It's time to grab your newspaper, your Bible, the spinach dip, and your girlfriends. It's time to encourage one another to dig deep in preparation to show Mama Bear to the world.

....

NOTES

[1]Lynne Hybels, *Nice Girls Don't Change the World* (Grand Rapids: Zondervan, 2005), 21. This is such an honest, inspiring book and a short read. Perfect for busy mamas looking for inspiration and growth.

[2] Shane Claiborne, *The Irresistible Revolution: Living as an Ordinary Radical* (Grand Rapids: Zondervan, 2006), 24. This book is a must-read. Run, don't walk, to the nearest bookstore or put down *Mama Bear* and hit up Amazon Prime. It lends itself well to group discussion.

[3] Lynne Hybels, quote about a small group of women changing the world.

CHAPTER THREE

Training in the Trenches

First find a path and a little light to see by.
Then push up your sleeves and start helping.
—**Anne Lamott**

Mama Bear takes the passion that lies within—the things that make her angry—and takes swift action. She is unafraid to attack the perceived danger and do everything in her power to protect her young. Propelled by the love of God, our feet, too, can move swiftly. We can guide our Mama Bear into a place of goodness beyond ourselves. We can harness our passion and our anger to make the dirty clean and the disenfranchised belong. As we worship a loving God and follow a Christ of kindness and peace, we might take that love and pour it into the things that keep us up at night.

In other words, we can push up our sleeves and put Mama Bear to work.

In order to do this, it is important for us to channel Mama Bear's passion in ways that suit us, that serve others, and that bring us joy. Just like we all have different angers and concerns, we also have different skills and talents. You might be the graceful hands of the body of Christ, whereas I might be a sturdy shoulder. All of us are necessary. Discovering our own area of strength, the ways in which we best operate, and how we are meant to serve is a soul-enriching experience. It can free us from what we need to be freed from and release us from the pressure that we put on ourselves.

As a part of an organized moms' group, I studied *Network: The Right People . . . In the Right Places . . . For the Right Reasons*, a book written to help individuals discover and utilize their spiritual gifts.[1] From this study, I learned that I do not possess the gift of administration. This was freeing to me. For many years, I had avoided my true colors and talked myself into an idea that I was efficient and organized—the kind of person who could fully comprehend or confidently create a complex master spreadsheet. I thought I was an administrator, even though my true fruits of the Spirit showed themselves in less structured ways.

When I learned this about myself, I was free to let go of the awkward expectation that I had placed on myself and begin to concentrate on my true, God-given gifts. I stopped pretending and began to work on being true to myself. I no longer volunteered to be the group organizer and released myself from the expectation that I should be. I forgave myself for the lack of joy and ease I experienced whenever I opened Excel. I then began to look for ways to implement and enjoy my stronger gifts, those of creative communication and encouragement. And guess what? I have been able to live more contentedly and have a much sharper idea of how I might serve the world and those around me.

In *The Purpose Driven Life*, Rick Warren reminds readers,

Each of us was uniquely designed by God with talents, gifts, skills, and abilities. The way you're "wired" is not an accident. God didn't give you your abilities for self-ish purposes. They were given to benefit others, just as others were given abilities for your benefit. The Bible says, "God has given gifts to each of you from his great variety of spiritual gifts. Manage them well so that God's generosity can flow through you. . . . Are you called to help others? Do it with all the strength and energy that God supplies. Then God will be given glory." (1 Pet. 4:10–11 NLT)[2]

Unlocking these gifts and talents is easier when you surround yourself with others as part of a life-giving community. With the encouragement and honesty of a trusted friend or group of friends, you can reflect on your gifts and work through prayer, study, and conversation to unlock the person God made you to be. You'll gain the confidence to finally release misplaced expectations and begin to operate in a much more authentic, enjoyable, fulfilling mode. It is when we understand ourselves, our passions, and our joys that we can truly take our Mama Bear and point her down a productive road or lead her in a just fight.

It is likely this advice is something you have reflected on in the past. You may have thought about this when considering a college major or looking for a job. Perhaps it has actually served you quite well in the workplace. However, motherhood changes things. It changes our perspectives and our lifestyles. Becoming a mother is the perfect time to reexamine ourselves as individuals. We can look for ways not only to use our true talents and gifts for our families and for the world, but also to seek action that brings us great satisfaction and personal joy.

Many of us come to motherhood as a "second career" of sorts. In so many ways, we are of a privileged generation living in a priv-ileged time and place. Many of us are well educated. Many of us have experienced great success in our careers outside the home. We are master teachers, specialists, scientists, entrepreneurs, and working artists. We have babies and, in some cases, are faced with the luxurious choice of whether or not to work outside the home at all and, if so, how much. This is a place of privilege that should be recognized.

For a lot of mamas today, it becomes quickly obvious that changing diapers, cleaning up drool, and enduring piercing cries is far less glamorous than hailing cabs, wearing heels, and expensing lunches. Nonetheless, millions of women work outside the home part-time, work from home, or enjoy some flexibility in their work roles so they can spend more time with their children. And millions more women are giving birth and staying put—giving up a career and second income, or working less outside of the home in order to witness their child's firsts. But as women sit in their offices, cubicles, or classrooms, still pregnant and daydreaming about their new life with babe, are they prepared for what is in store?

When my husband and I were expecting our first child, we decided together that I would quit my job as a high school English teacher and stay at home full-time with the baby. I'll be honest: I had visions of reading great books with a cup of coffee in my hand and a bundle of babe in my lap. I saw myself dressed in my pre-pregnancy best. I envisioned my child next to me in the kitchen, sitting happily in his infant chair, cooing and batting at the toys dangling in front of him while I prepared a healthy lunch.

What I didn't expect was to go days without showering, to order in every other night, and to clean only when I knew someone was coming over (if that). The truth is, I personally found it much more challenging to be at home taking care of one baby boy than to be teaching nearly one hundred teenagers each day. Part of the problem was that there were many times when I felt lonely. My coworkers had vanished. My newborn "boss" was demanding and he spoke a language that was completely foreign. And the job was beyond full-time—I worked day and night, got dirty, and was often confronted with way too many unpleasant smells.

I missed using different parts of my brain. I missed grading papers and talking about classic literature with curious students. Though I loved being able to be at home with Oliver, I often felt that I had more to say and more to give to the larger world. Though I carried the overwhelming belief that my son had come into the world for a reason and that God had chosen me to be his mother for a specific purpose, I questioned what had happened to the life I once knew. I also sensed potential for the time of transition to be a time of growth.

Many of us who find ourselves staying at home with our children are happy to embrace other outlets and reignite the "other" part of our mother selves. Doing so is not only healthy, but also necessary. I remember a friend saying that she felt like she was a better mother to her young children after she came home from the ten hours of work that she was able to do outside her home each week. She spent a portion of her energy in a much different capacity, which filled her up.

Rachel Iverson is a thoughtful writer who once wrote a column called "Mother and Other" for the webzine *Literary Mama*. It's important, she says week after week, to allow our "other" self to coexist with our "mother" self. She writes the following in an essay entitled "Going on a Rachel Hunt":

So who are we anyway? Mothers, definitely. But we're still people, too, aren't we? Sometimes it's hard to tell. When I'm foraging in the depths of my kitchen cupboards for a clean sippy cup while holding a whining seven-month-old on my hip and trying not to step on the whining three-and-a-half-year-old sprawled on the dirty tile floor, it's really hard to tell. I've been a Mommy for three and a half years and that's not very long compared to the thirty-three and a half years that I've been Rachel. But Mommy has been known to swallow Rachel whole.[3]

If you find yourself in the situation in which you are not holding down a time-consuming job outside of the home and are spending your hours at home with your children, or if you are simply baffled by your new role as a mom, you might experience a longing for your "other" self. While we enjoy our role as mothers, embrace it with our whole hearts, and likely feel grateful for the opportunity, we cannot deny that there are other parts of our rich identities. Our loving and creative God made us to be complex creatures with beautiful, far-reaching purpose.

If we start to forget, we need to go on a hunt for ourselves, just as Iverson suggests. Iverson ultimately found herself at the bookstore, in crossword puzzles, and at the movies. A lawyer in her "previous" life, she felt that a part of herself had been exorcised since having children, and she worked to bring a different pocket of her brain back to life.

Perhaps we need to revert back to our high school career fair and ask ourselves the questions that our counselors posed. Keeping in mind, however, that just as our hairstyle has likely changed, our purpose and mission may be different as well. At this point in our lives, we may not be pointing toward a new career in the workforce, but rather reflecting on what makes our "other self" tick. Discovering what we are made for will allow our "mother" selves and our "other" selves to bloom and blossom. (Not to mention our "friend" self, our "spouse" self, our "daughter" and "sister" self, and so on.) It will also help focus our Mama Bears when the time is right.

So go ahead and ask yourself: When do I feel most alive? Is it at the bookstore? Is it when I'm planning and preparing dinner for friends? Perhaps you love a good spreadsheet. Maybe you have great affection for the written word. Do you love running? What makes your heart pound and your soul feel refreshed?

Your joy is no coincidence. God gave each of us unique passions and ways in which to feel fully alive in his creation. In her memoir *Traveling Mercies*, writer Anne Lamott writes about the things she loves and the things she lives in. "I live in joy and motion and cover-ups. I live in the nourishment of food and the sun and the warmth of the people who love me," she says.[4]

As moms, we have to continually ask the question: What do I live in? We might actually need a nudge (cue the Pinot and purposeful conversations) in order to rediscover such things. If we don't take a moment for a bit of self-reflection between pouring cereal, tying shoes, kissing owies, coordinating schedules, and all of the other thousands of tasks we tackle throughout the day, we run the risk of forgetting the essence of ourselves, which favors no one.

It is during these moments that we rekindle our innate, God-given passions and joys. And not only do we do so to feed ourselves, but we do it so that we can prepare to serve those around us more fully. The beauty is in the fact that we can take our very essence— the things that we are gifted in and the things that we live in—and turn it into our best weapon. Our joy becomes the joy of others. Our joy becomes Mama Bear's action.

This is where I've found that things can get dramatic and life-changing. This is the part where your purpose gets bigger, your life gets fuller, and your joy grows exponentially.

Find your joy and let Mama Bear channel it. Identify the things that make you angry and the things that make you move. This is the moment that you get creative in your response to the world. This is when giving back and living like a mama on a mission becomes increasingly fulfilling. Train your Mama Bear to use your joy as the rocket-fuel response to her anger. Take your gifts—the things that you love doing the most and that bring joy and satisfaction to your soul—and do them in response to the thing that makes your blood boil. As Frances Buechner writes in *Wishful Thinking: A Seeker's ABC*, "The place God calls you is the place where your deep gladness and the world's deep hunger meet."[5] This is the land where Mama Bear lumbers powerfully toward goodness in ways you find exhilarating and fun.

My good friend Beth has four children. Though she has a master's degree and worked with children with physical and mental disabilities in Chicago for many years, Beth traded a career to stay home and raise her children, all of whom she homeschools. Beth is a beautiful writer and thinker. She and her husband are Orthodox Christians and have been active in establishing a church in the small city she calls home. Beth also happens to be an outstanding baker. She loves to bake and does so with amazing results. (It is my sincere hope that you have a thoughtful, generous baker friend in your life.)

Since I first met Beth as part of a book club years ago, there have been times when she knew I was struggling. During these dark moments, Beth has provided light in the form of sugar, yeast, and flour. Have you ever experienced the pleasure of pulling up to your home to find a dozen chocolate-chunk cookies or a loaf of freshly baked bread waiting on your porch? Her small gestures of love are an earthly hug from heaven.

Did Beth go out of her way to help her friend? Yes. It is no small thing to bundle up four children in the midst of a Midwestern winter, pile them in the minivan, and drive across town to make a delivery to a friend. But did she derive some personal pleasure in the act of baking for her hurting friend? Absolutely. Beth has told me that some of her best time is spent in her kitchen. "I may never write a book or start a charity or do anything notably 'big' with my life. But I can definitely set a table for a meal," she has said.

By preparing and delivering food to people in need, Beth is clearly embodying the living Christ. She has taken an act that she loves—cooking—and is using her gift to make the world a little sweeter.

One thing that makes the wise, thoughtful, beautiful Beth angry is that not everyone in this world has access to clean water. She has traveled extensively and is pained by the sorrows of the world. The lack of clean water is something that she has both studied and witnessed firsthand and it makes her blood boil. So, for the last six Novembers, her small kitchen has become her battleground. She has called to mind the pictures she's seen, the facts she's learned, and the experiences she has had through her travels to the impoverished areas of the earth. She has allowed herself to feel angry about this injustice and she has sharply focused her reaction. In the second week of November, Beth frees her Mama Bear from captivity. She tucks her small children into bed, pours herself a glass of Cabernet, and bares her claws. Beth—wife, friend, sister, mother of four, and trained Mama Bear—does something beautiful. She makes fudge. *Hundreds* of servings of fudge. Then she packs it up in her minivan, and she serves it at a local fundraising party where each year thousands of dollars are raised to build or repair freshwater wells in the places people live without this basic human need.

Beth's spirit reminds me of that of Saint Therese of Lisieux. She writes of such love in her "Little Way," as it came to be known, and which is explained in her autobiography, *Story of a Soul.* "Love proves itself by deeds, so how am I to show my love? Great deeds are forbidden me," wrote Sister Therese in 1897 from her Carmelite convent in France. "The only way I can prove my love is by . . . every little sacrifice, every glance and word, and the doing of the least actions for love."[6]

My friend Vicky will tell you that two of her great loves in life are her family and this season's fashion. One of the most down-to-earth people I know, she loves *People* magazine, reality television, and looking great. Vicky is also ridiculously caring and compassionate. Here's an example of her heart: one afternoon several of us mamas and a couple of our kids were hanging out at her house and had migrated to her room. We were all admiring this season's shoes and bags and oohing and ahhing over her great taste.

"Do you like those?" she said to our friend Jen, who was ogling a pair of shoes.

"Um, yes!" squealed Jen. "They're adorable!"

Without skipping a beat, Vicky smiled and said, "Take them! Seriously. Keep 'em."

To Tasha, who was petting a purse: "That bag? Really? It's yours," Vicky said.

And so on. We laughed and talked and stroked her wardrobe and Vicky just kept giving her clothes away. If we didn't know her so well, we might have been slightly awed. But that's Vicky. She is as loving and generous as they come.

That's why it didn't surprise me at all when Vicky spoke of befriending a young couple in her church.

"I know this sounds weird since I've never really met you," she said to a young woman after a Sunday morning service. "But you have a little boy just a bit younger than my son, Ethan, so I'm going to be giving you all of Ethan's old clothes from now on."

Though I wasn't there to see it, I can imagine the conversation. Vicky, marching up in her six-inch platforms and cute jeans, blonde ponytail bobbing along the way. The woman being handed a bag of little-boy clothing, beaming. Vicky uses her unique gifts to love other people. Her light is bright . . . and always in the season's hottest color.

"Do small things with great love." That's what Mother Teresa tells us, and that's what Vicky, with an *Us Weekly* tucked into this season's bag, does. She has a God-given ability to make people feel special and to offer dignity to her fellow humans. Vicky wouldn't admit it if you asked her, but I wouldn't be surprised if someday she figures out a way to clothe an entire shelter of battered women or shoe an entire village of children. She's got a Mama Bear who could effortlessly—and with great energy, style, and charm—change the world.

I consider the acts of kindness and generosity exhibited by these women to be pure acts of worship. So often we think that serving God requires great sacrifice and discomfort. Sometimes it does. Sometimes we have to change behavior and strive for renewal in ways that are uncomfortable or inconvenient. But that's not the bulk of what God requires. In Matthew, Jesus separates the goats and the sheep, inviting the sheep into the kingdom of God for their love and care of the "least of these" and condemning the goats for their inaction. Addressing the sheep, he says this:

> "For I was hungry and you gave me something to eat, I was thirsty and you gave me something to drink, I was a stranger and you invited me in, I needed clothes and you clothed me, I was sick and you looked after me, I was in prison and you came to visit me." Then the righteous will answer him, "Lord, when did we see you hungry and feed you, or thirsty and give you something to drink? When did we see you a stranger and invite you in, or needing clothes and clothe you? When did we see you sick or in prison and go to visit you?" The King will reply, "Truly I tell you, whatever you did for one of the least of these brothers and sisters of mine, you did for me." (Matt. 25:35–40)

Jesus minces no words in this intense story. Hearing it always makes me nervous and yet excited. Nervous because he doesn't tell us exactly how each of us should proceed after hearing it. There is no detailed to-do list for the twenty-first-century mother included in the story. Rather, he leaves it up to us to figure out how best to care for our brothers and sisters. What's exciting is that he knows each of us was created with incredible gifts and talents. He recognizes us as creative, resourceful beings and expects us to use these traits to feed, shoe, shelter, and care for "the least of these."

As mothers, I hope we have the vision to see that changing a diaper is a loving and worthy calling and that the face of Jesus is in our helpless infant. Packing lunches and preparing snacks for our children are sacred tasks. These are worthy roles that we are in the unique position to fulfill. Often we fall into believing that the only place that needs our act of service is the soup kitchen. And though your local soup kitchen would probably not turn away your offer to help, there is much more to be done and the world is rich with possibility. What if you have small children and no sitter and find it impossible to wield a ladle with kids underfoot? What if you're an introvert who doesn't enjoy cooking or baking? Our ideas about how to serve should not be limited. God has gifted you in unique ways, and with a little creativity and resourcefulness those gifts can be used by Mama Bear to teach compassion and relieve suffering. Practice lovingkindness at home and then look for ways to spend yourself with the same passion and tenderness beyond your backyard.

The space in which our passions, pleasures, and talents take shape and become outwardly productive is our sweet spot. In the professional world, we might look for this in the work we are paid to do. We can also find our sweet spot in the ways in which we serve our community and the world around us as new mothers. Many of us find ourselves anxious to use the skills that we once used in the workplace. We are simply trying to find a way to plug them into our new lives with children. I am always amazed at the ways in which mothers identify their anger, their joy, and their skill, and then use the combination to love the world. So many among us are reshaping the present in creative ways that nourish souls, all the while providing incredible examples for children, and living out the calling to love neighbors near and far.

Recently, I walked into my local coffee shop and discovered a large display of beautiful, handcrafted jewelry. Each piece of jewelry was unique—stones and cylinders in earthy colors—and very attractive. I was drawn in by the overall style and quality of the work. When I looked for a price (everything was marked at ten dollars), I found that all proceeds from the sale of the jewelry would go to an organization working to end all forms of child slavery and exploitation.

A creative barista used the tips from her part-time coffee shop job to buy supplies for her work and then used her artistic gift to help others. The owners of Dunn Bros. Coffee allowed her to prominently display her jewelry and to sell it in their store. People fawned over the goods and were inspired by her generous, creative spirit. To date, she has channeled her outrage and used her talent to raise two thousand dollars for the organization Love 146.

My friend Jen is an incredible artist and Kim is a thoughtful blogger. Jen, mother of two boys in elementary school, reclaims old material and makes it beautiful by styling and hand painting unique signs for businesses and homes. Kim, mother of a toddler, writes about her home-improvement adventures (she and her husband just built their own house!) on her popular lifestyle blog.[7] When these two women sensed a local need, they went to work using their collective talents to raise money for Dress for Success, an organization working to promote the economic independence of disadvantaged women by providing professional attire, a network of support, and career development.

Jen and Kim teamed up to host a sign-painting workshop for local crafters and home improvers. They donated the supplies, provided refreshments, took the time to plan the event, and then used the admission they charged to support other women through Dress for Success. In everything she does, Jen strives for beauty. Kim uses her communications and event-planning know-how to encourage others and inspire good. These women have big hearts and sound skills. They used their great passion to provide women in their community with dignity and opportunity. They uncovered great personal joy in doing so.

A few months ago, I was lucky enough to personally benefit from my friend Jennie's extraordinary passion and talent. Jennie is a busy mom to three young children. Her husband works full-time as an emergency room nurse and, to supplement their income and practice her passion, Jennie runs a photography business in our community. Several months ago, Jennie decided to use her love of photography to raise money for The Adventure Project, a non-profit organization working to bring dignity and jobs to men and women across the globe. (The Adventure Project has become one of my favorite organizations; 10 percent of my royalties from the purchase of this book will be directed to their efforts. Thank you!)

On her personal blog, Jennie wrote with great enthusiasm about her belief in The Adventure Project and encouraged her readers to further their cause by donating twenty dollars to their mission. As an incentive, she promised each donor a chance to win a family photo shoot. Because I was moved by her passion and her words and because I would love the chance to be photographed by this talented woman, I donated twenty dollars and hoped for the best. A few weeks later, she drew my name out of a hat. My family had a great time posing for photographs, and we were delighted with Jennie's work, but we were also thrilled by the knowledge that Jennie's contest had raised hundreds of dollars for The Adventure Project.

My mother-in-law is a fabric artist. Not only does she sew (she made my wedding dress and my groom's navy blue tuxedo), but she makes portraits out of thread. What began as a hobby many years ago could be a full-time job for Terre. However, she makes charity a priority. Anytime there is an opportunity to donate her work, Terre is the first to sign up. Her work has covered dozens of service men and women through a program call Quilts of Valor, which strives to provide any and all veterans touched by war with the warmth and healing power of a quilt. She takes the joy she finds in the hum of the sewing machine and uses it as a way to serve her neighbors. As she works, she meditates over her creation, pouring out positive energy into the person whom the fabric will some-day touch. She prays for the person who might pass by the thread painting each day as it hangs in her living room and the individ-ual who feels soft fabric against his skin. Her God-given talent is used as an acknowledgment of suffering in the world.

After discovering the ease of making bath salts and the relax-ation the product provided (who can argue with a relaxing bath at the end of the day?), I decided that, with the help of some friends, I could use my new craft obsession as a fundraising effort for one of my favorite charities. I bought supplies in bulk, gathered some girlfriends, and enjoyed a Monday-night crafting party. We even-tually sold the salts and raised nine hundred dollars. And we had a great time doing it.

Stirring together sea salt and essential oil, photographing friends, and creating quilts quickly become acts of worship when your motions are made for the kingdom. What all of these examples have in common is that each woman has evaluated her strengths and passions and has found a pathway to God. When we talk about worship, we often think of the songs that we sing on Sunday morn-ings with the praise and worship band. But worship is so much more than that. As Mark Batterson writes in his book *Primal*, "I know God loves the sound of our voices when we sing songs of praise. It's music to his ears. But you know what God loves even more? God loves the smell of your sweat. . . . God loves it when we break a sweat serving his purposes. Our energy turns into beautiful melodies."[8]

Examples of creative worship are everywhere. You'll see more later in the book when I describe the Water for Christmas effort that took root in my community. Though I like to think I know some pretty extraordinary people, the truth is that your circle of friends is probably much like mine. The short examples of love and worship in this chapter are the acts of everyday people. They are actions made by moms who spend the majority of their days taking care of children. However, these women have found that they have a bit of extra energy to spend, and they have made pouring their love out into the world a priority. They are personally fulfilled in return. The Mama Bear they hold deep inside has become riled up over a sensed injustice, and these women have responded in a way that brings them great joy. They are women with a Bible in one hand and a newspaper in another. They are aware of the brokenness of the world and yet have seen God's love and thus used their blessings and great love to shine their light. As the mystic poet Rumi says, "Let the beauty of what you love be what you do. There are a thousand ways to kneel and kiss the ground."

So what's your great joy? What's the beauty that you notice and love? And how can you use it, as Buechner says, to ease the hunger pangs of the world? God made each of us as unique individuals with beautiful talents all of our own. How can you leverage your love for the kingdom? Perhaps discussion with your moms' group will help you discover ways in which you can kneel and kiss the ground. Loving the world joyfully and abundantly does not stem from guilt or obligation or duty. Authentic service stems from the pouring out of spirit and pleasure and love.

Your service to God will be one of great joy. You'll feel an energy and a passion that can only come from something bigger than yourself. You'll stay up late designing attractive packaging or writing passionate blog posts. You'll use the pure gold of naptime to craft jewelry or make phone calls. You'll fall into bed simultaneously exhausted and energized. You'll have given all of your love away and fall asleep with a sweet smile on your lips. Mama Bear's anger will be channeled for good. "The person born with a talent they are meant to use will find their greatest happiness in using it," says writer and poet Johann Wolfgang von Goethe.

Using your position of motherhood and training Mama Bear will begin a practice in the way you think about the world. Nurturing Mama Bear provides a new perspective that asks us to look outside of ourselves. If we allow it to, intentionally practicing our response to anger by channeling our gratefulness and joy will spill into everything we do. We'll begin to take our creativity and get more creative. Not only is the shift of perspective life-changing, but also such a way of life is magnetic. It's contagious. You'll start to notice and be inspired by friends who have trained their Mama Bears. People might start to notice you.

And what's one thing that's better than a lone Mama Bear responding to her intense anger with her great joy? A slew of Mamas with pushed-up sleeves looking for trouble and responding with tremendous creativity and astonishing love.

....

NOTES

[1]Bruce Bugbee, Don Cousins, and Bill Hybels, *Network: The Right People . . . In the Right Places . . . For the Right Reasons* (Grand Rapids: Zondervan, 2004). Another survey of giftedness is the Gallup Strengthsfinder at https://www .gallupstrengthscenter.com. You get your top five strengths for fifteen dollars, so

depending on your budget, this would be fun to discuss. Instead of going out to dinner, Jake and I did this as an at-home date night.

[2] Rick Warren, *The Purpose Driven Life* (Grand Rapids: Zondervan, 2002), 57. I first read this book at my mother's suggestion. Jake and I completed the study together, and I've since done it a few times on my own. I've found it to be a nice Lenten study to complete on my own.

[3] Rachel Iverson, "Going on a Rachel Hunt," Mother and Other column, *Literary Mama*, December 2003, www.literarymama.com/columns /motherandother/archives/2003/12/going-on-a-rachel-hunt.html.

[4] Anne Lamott, *Traveling Mercies: Some Thoughts on Faith* (New York: Pantheon Books, 2005), 197.

[5] Frances Buechner, *Wishful Thinking: A Seeker's ABC* (New York: HarperCollins, 1993), 19.

[6] Saint Therese of Lisieux, *Story of a Soul* (Washington, D.C.: ICS Publications, 1996). I first heard about this book and read this quote while enjoying *The Happiness Project* by Gretchen Rubin (New York: HarperCollins, 2009), 212.

[7] Newlywoodwards.com; quadcities.dressforsuccess.org.

[8] Mark Batterson, *Primal* (New York: Random House, 2009), 134.

PART TWO

Compared with other carnivores, bears
walk slowly and deliberately,
with all five toes as well as their heels
touching the ground. They can, however,
move quickly if the need arises.

—The Smithsonian's Animal Encyclopedia

CHAPTER FOUR

Living and Loving Out Loud

God appoints our graces to be nurses
to other men's weaknesses.
—Henry Ward Beecher

As you establish relationships within the group through study, conversation, and prayer, you'll gather momentum as a small community of God-loving, baby-wearing, toddler-chasing, or middle-school-surviving women. When you arrive at this level of comfort and relationship, you may feel inclined to begin conversations about what to do with your momentum. How might the Spirit move among you? How might you take your talents and your Mama Bear anger, join together, and put yourselves to work? How might you use this powerful mama force that you have access to within your group?

This missional urge may come about naturally in your conversation with one another. It may grow organically during a book discussion or a Bible study. Perhaps you'll feel the fire during a playdate at the park. Maybe you'll hear about an organization or learn about an ache in the world and feel moved to take it to your circle of confidants for consideration. It may simply be a matter of focusing conversation and bringing your vision to the table. We want to use our gifts and love those around us. Sometimes it just takes someone or something to start the engine or provide the nudge. So how might one begin?

I once had the opportunity to ask Sheryl WuDunn, who co-authored *Half the Sky* and *A Path Appears* with her husband Nicholas Kristof (for details about each, turn to the Fuel for Your Fire section at the end of this book), this question: I see overwhelming injustice around me and I don't want to sit still. Where do I start?

WuDunn, who had just finished her keynote address on the subject of women and social justice, was clear in her response. "Find what you're passionate about and get together with your friends. It's more fun that way. Decide *where* you want to work or *what* you want to work on, and then find an organization who is doing that work in the world. Use the things you're good at and the things you enjoy to make a change."

I wholeheartedly agree with this advice. I also believe there's a first step to take once you've gathered your group. Similar to self-care, it's necessary to love one another well. We need to be good friends to each other and this requires deliberate nurturing. There are many ways to make your moms' group start to move, and you may be anxious to jump into an intense brainstorming session with your mamas to try to figure out what your mission in your community and the world might be. However, we can't forget that loving service is a discipline that requires thoughtful intentions and daily practice. That's why it's important to recognize the brilliant opportunity we have to make sure we're caring for one another within our moms' group before rushing out to offer hearts and hands to the rest of the world. Taking care of one another is not only an important part of being in community, but it's also a great way to flex your muscles before (and during) the big event.

There's a common anecdote for those who neglect self-care and instead sacrifice themselves in potentially unhealthy ways. It centers very dramatically on a travel nightmare: the plane that you're on is going down. We were instructed preflight to secure our own oxygen masks before helping those around us, even if the one seated next to us is a child. Such instructions may go against our nature, especially as mamas looking after our cubs. But we are given these instructions because, without oxygen of our own, we are no good to anyone else. If we are panting and wheezing because we're busy taking care of those around us, our service is shallow and will soon expire. However, if we fit our own oxygen mask first, taking care of our most primary need of that moment, we will be strong and ready to jump to action.

The example is extreme. Your moms' group is not in any imminent danger of falling from the sky. However, it's still important to take care of one another and to get into the practice of serving those you love in real and tangible ways before extending the intention to others. This lumbering toward action beginning within your small circle of women will help you discover your gifts and talents and where your sweet spot lies. You might learn that your impulse is to feed people. Or maybe you'll realize the truth that you can find joy in organizational tasks. You might discover the areas that you lean toward when called upon to help. It might also help you realize that you can do hard, inconvenient things for other people and experience satisfaction in the action. Taking care of those in your immediate community benefits everyone and, ultimately, those involved will find that there is indeed something contagious about doing good.

Sometimes it simply takes one person to do something simple to inspire the rest of us. The other day, my friend Becky brought pita chips and hummus to a group meeting and spread it out on the table to share. It was delightful . . . and so simple. It was just the boost I needed in the middle of that long day. Her small act of kindness (going to the grocery before coming over or maybe even just pillaging her cupboard for the treat) made those at the table smile and feel loved. My friend Jen made my day by dropping off a plant on my first day in a new office space.

One day, as I was sitting in a coffee shop feeling rather sad and overwhelmed, a woman in her seventies approached my table and told me I was "adorable." I was not feeling very adorable that day and her words of affirmation completely changed my mood. Even something as simple as a text message of support can make you feel loved and cared for. I'm anxious to pay these actions forward the next time I get the chance. After being the recipient of such thoughtfulness, I try to take every opportunity to spread kindness. See a woman rocking a pregnant belly? Tell her a kind word. Witness a mom struggling with her toddler in the middle of Target? Give her a knowing and compassionate smile. Notice someone struggling with the door? Get up and help. Don't squander these simple moments of outward love.

As a group, we can adhere to the phrase popular on T-shirts and bumper stickers in the 1980s: Practice Random Acts of Kindness and Senseless Acts of Beauty. We can start small and warm up the engines. The offer to babysit in a pinch or bake cupcakes for a frazzled mama planning a party will mean something. These kind gestures will resonate. Selfless love is a thing of beauty that will resound deeply within your circle of friends. Make action a practice and you'll witness its ripple effect.

Here is an example of one way that a small kindness rippled through my community of moms: when our second son, Elihu, was born shortly after Christmas, my friend Christina visited me in the hospital. She had a little one at home and was just weeks away from having a new baby herself, but she took the time to trudge through the city traffic and the snow and will her pregnant body up the stairs to the hospital room where I was resting. She carried with her a bag from Whole Foods. The bag held a beautiful mix of berries—strawberries, raspberries, blackberries—lush and delicious. There was also a small bottle of Naked Green Machine juice and an organic peanut butter rice crispy bar. This delivery was a far cry from the hospital food I had been eating. I was touched that she would take the time to nourish my body with this thoughtful gift of food just after I gave birth.

Her love was tangible in her action and I found it both energizing and contagious. Since then, I have been inspired by Christina's action and have blatantly borrowed her brilliance, showing up for a brief hospital visit to other postpartum friends, sharing fresh food and the sentiment of nourishment and healing and embracing a time in which a woman should be pampered. It is with incredible pleasure that I do my best to show up and take part in these moments.

Also inspired by Christina's generosity and care for my physical being during this one moment in time, I partnered with my friend Cathy to give a healthy-cooking demonstration geared toward mothers with young children at the local farmers' market. We handed out food, recipes, collective wisdom, and cookbooks and enjoyed a beautiful morning of food, community, and conversation. We worked hard on this event, but we enjoyed ourselves and reaped benefit in our service. As so many psychologists are finding, the best thing we can do to bump up our own happiness is to do something for someone else. Christina's errand to Prentice Women's Hospital years ago has ultimately impacted a larger community of women. It inspired me to be the change I wanted to see.

When you belong to a community and you groom true and authentic relationships, the benefits are astounding. Of course, such friendship does not happen overnight. There is work involved in establishing the trust and commitment that's involved. It requires showing up and bringing your true self. It requires honesty and vulnerability. It requires paying attention to one another and really looking each other in the eye. It requires silencing the smartphone as well as the loop of things to do running through your mind. It requires the work of and the investment in a real relationship: the time commitment, the attention, and the free exchange of grace.

But then, because of all of this pleasure and struggle and conflict and joy, our relationships become a testament to the moment that Jesus refers to when he talks about sitting down to a banquet in the kingdom of heaven. The work has been done, the food prepared. The humble and beautiful have taken their seats. Bellies are filled and pleasure ensues. Have you ever had those moments when you think: this is all that my little brain can grasp as heaven? Maybe you're sitting at a long table with a glass of wine in your hand and perfectly prepared pasta on your plate. Maybe you're at a baseball game or you're walking through the woods. What do you see when you catch a glimpse of God or a peek at heaven? It's likely that in these most beautiful moments you're not alone. It's likely that the experience is communal and you're enjoying the peace and pleasure of the moment with the ones that you love.

True community is like that, but only because you've already put in the work. You know that behind the smiles, there was heartache and then triumph. You know that the setting is only what it is because of the hard work it took to get there. This is the work of getting to know one another, of serving one another, and then celebrating together. We understand joy better when we've experienced pain and when we've invested the necessary time and tender love that comes with building authentic community. It's after we've served one another and loved one another that we can enjoy the sweetness of friendship. You were made in God's image and your capacity to love is astounding.

Did I mention that I continued to eat well after we left the hospital with Elihu? One of the women in our little moms' posse with a huge heart and seemingly enormous energy began to organize meals for new parents in our larger church community. A former employee of the Chicago mayor's office, this woman knows how to get things done. By the time Elihu was born, a care ministry was in full swing and we reaped amazing benefits. For three full weeks, every other evening a kind soul—more often than not it was one of my "mom friends" or their husbands—arrived at our apartment door with a hot meal tucked into a basket or a bag. We ate pasta, roasted chicken, and homemade tortillas. We were treated to veggie stir-fry, fresh mesclun salads, and beautiful desserts. In other words, we ate like royalty without lifting a finger. The generosity was truly outrageous and is an example of the ripple effect and how we can move in ways that might matter to one another. It may not have seemed like much to each individual preparing the meal, but to us it meant less time cooking and more time cuddling our new babe. It meant nutrition for my healing, life-giving body. It meant chatting at the door and the opportunity to show off our son. It meant huge savings in our grocery budget that we were able to reallocate to other places. It meant love and prayers over our family. A glimpse of heaven, it meant the world to us.

Receiving such kindness changes a person and inspires her to be better. Since being shown this culinary love, I try to do better myself. I understand the blessing because I've received it too. A lost job means a pot of soup. A sick child in the middle of a long winter warrants a sweet treat. A promotion or positive life event should be marked by a bottle of wine. Trust me when I say that I owe the universe a whole lot of lasagna.

But your community of moms will not just be about offering food. When I got sick and had to undergo a long battery of tests, it was Holly who swooped in and cared for my toddler. When one of us was struggling with her marriage, it was Melissa who lent hours of wisdom and counsel before we all circled in prayer. For as many times as Emily and I have clinked glasses in celebration, we've shared pressing concerns and worked hard at understanding one another. I've learned from those around me that caring for one another is about a ride to the airport. It's about showing up with flowers on the anniversary of a loved one's death. It's sending a note of encouragement when you hear the tremor of pain in someone's voice and popping the champagne when there's something to celebrate. It's about showing up and being ready to invest. It's about, as Kanye says, *being* the roses.[1]

Being the recipient of such generosity and love also serves as a reminder that we can't, in fact, do it alone. Or it at least gives us a poke as if to say life is better when we *don't have to* do it alone. Sharing pain and pleasure with someone else lessens the burden and broadens the joy. In a world where we are increasingly self-reliant and kept separate from one another by our literal and figurative fences, letting others help is humbling and is a clear reminder that life—even the vulnerable and ugly parts—is better when shared.

I write this assuming that you're reading this book alongside a group of women or with your tribe of friends in mind. However, I understand that cultivating community is really, *really* hard and, depending on your circumstances, you might read these examples of love and compassion and feel a deep sense of sadness and longing. As human beings we crave beautiful and authentic connection, but there are spells of life that feel dry and are void of what we're built for. It takes time to find friendship and then time to deepen new relationships. When you find that you're the new girl in town or that your life circumstances have changed dramatically (for instance, you become a mom!), you need to get brave and step up to the plate. Think back on the important relationships you've enjoyed over the course of your life and you'll quickly realize that life-giving friendship and deep camaraderie don't develop overnight. Persistence is required.

Developing healthy community and rich relationships requires an element of bravery. As I mentioned in the introduction, I was more than nervous to take Veronica up on her invitation to start a moms' group at our church. I had already tried two local moms' groups—one hosted at a church other than the one I attended and one at a venue focused solely on connecting moms. I had been trying to develop friendships with several women I had met, but was frankly weary of "first playdates" and awkward conversations. I was lonely and flat-out desperate when Veronica reached out to me. I was afraid, but I also had an instinctive understanding that connecting with other women going through the experience of new motherhood would be worth the initial discomfort. I said yes to her invitation, put one foot in front of the other, and showed up.

Finding your tribe of Mama Bears can be scary and uncomfortable, but it takes showing up. It takes being willing to feel uncomfortable and awkward. I have experienced this deep longing for camaraderie over and over again with each move to a new place or new phase of life. Again and again, in acts of sheer boldness and with a determination that has sometimes surprised me, I've forced myself to go to the meeting, attend the event, enter the room, or join the conversation, even though I didn't know a soul. I trust you will, too. Good friends come from engaging in reflective conversations at parks; good friends come from going to book clubs you don't really feel like attending, because you have the wherewithal to know you need a night out of the house; good friends come from responding to a flyer advertising an event in your community that appeals to you; good friends come from taking a chance and saying hi to the woman pushing a stroller that you keep running into at your local coffee shop.

Of course there are magical moments in life when friendships just seem to "click," but it is more likely that it will take a beat of tremendous courage and months of discovery and deliberate trust building to fully reap the benefits of companionship and kinship. Don't give up, Mama Bear. Your people are out there. Summon your strength, open your ever-patient heart, and go find them.

When you boldly step into that circle and begin to love and trust your sisters, release a breath of thanks for the gift. And when you arrive at such a life-giving community, allow it to nudge you toward considering your role in the larger world.

If part of our purpose is to help and support and serve, it's also important to understand what it feels like to be on the receiving side of the blessing. Letting others serve us is humbling and beautiful. Appearing vulnerable and in need of help puts us in a different sort of posture and helps us to remember that all of us are doing the best we can, and none of us is too perfect, too put-together, or too competent to be beyond the need for the love and care of others.

We need one another. And thankfully, once established, you and your community of women are in this together. With each other's support, you should strive to live lives full of love and service. You'll need the others to cheer you on. You'll need the momentum of the group and you'll need some inspiration. God designed us to be in dynamic community with one another. Not only is this a gift, but it's also an opportunity to grow in your understanding of God, better know yourself, and more fully live the gospel of Christ.

It's also science. Recently, there has been all kinds of research done on the human capacity for happiness, and much of it is finding that happiness is a cycle that goes around and around. When we see someone help another person (or are helped ourselves), it gives us a good feeling and in turn causes us to go out and do something altruistic. As we reshape the way we think about relationships, communities, and what small groups of people are capable of, spreading love will become easier and more automatic. Your impulse to move your hands and feet for the kingdom will become the one you feel first. And you'll probably find that life will become more enjoyable. It often seems that the giver receives the first gift.

Ultimately, your experience of carefully cultivated community will be filled with these small acts of kindness buoyed by God's love. And these lovely, vulnerable, inspiring moments of friendship will set the foundation for bigger and bolder waves. The practice of kindness and love in action commandeered by you and your girlfriends just might usher in a revolution of love for which you—and the rest of the world—are aching.

. . . .

NOTE

[1]Kanye West, "Roses," *Late Registration,* Def Jam Recordings, 2005, mp3.

CHAPTER FIVE

Protecting through Prayer

There is not in the world a kind of life more sweet and
delightful than that of a continual conversation with God.

—Brother Lawrence

What will separate you from your neighborhood playgroup or the PTA is that your group is gathering as self-professed God-loving women. This certainly doesn't mean that all groups can't be socially involved and work toward the greater good. However, when you proclaim a faith centered on the actions and teachings of Christ, you follow the guide of the Bible, a book that repeatedly instructs us to intentionally, dutifully, and joyfully spill love out into the world. This shared understanding alone will change the group dynamic.

Let's be honest: channeling Mama Bear and working for good is a bold task, a task in which you're going to need the power and protection of God. From the beginning, the Church of Wrigleyville moms' group was intentional about communal prayer. Some of us were braver than others about voicing our prayers aloud (more on that later), but each week we set the tone of our group meeting by inviting God to be a part of it. We boldly petitioned God to be present in the room where we were gathered and asked that our conversations be guided by our higher power.

The fruit of this was not only in the depth of our discussions but also in the quickened bonds of friendship that praying with and for one another produced. There is something about praying together as a group and praying for one another that helps to form a deeper level of friendship. If you have never experienced this before, try it and you'll soon understand and be amazed at the way God can work in a community that values prayer and puts time into it.

Praying with a community can be beneficial in many ways. We can learn a lot from one another about the act of praying itself. When I was a child, my mother insisted on praying together before bed each and every night. This habit of my childhood is one that I have kept. But in my twenties, I began praying more than just before bed. I heard a sermon about maintaining a "prayerful spirit"—one in which you are constantly praying. God, I heard the priest say as I sat in a wooden pew, could always be on your mind, just under the surface of whatever task or joy or challenge you were facing. Really? I wondered. How can this be?

This was a life-changing message for me that reminded me of God's unceasing care and presence. I was in awe of the idea that we could constantly be engaged with God, even while experiencing the mundane. I was energized by the idea that I could be in conversation with God not just before I fell asleep at night, but all day long—before big moments and small. These conversations could take place not just on my knees at the foot of my bed, but on the subway or in the checkout line. I could walk down the street and acknowledge God in the breeze and the birds. I could open a book and open myself to the flow of love within each word. I could be folding laundry or washing a dish and meditate on the act of doing so and on God's hand in the moment. Though revolutionary to me as a twenty-two-year-old, this is not a new idea. "Rejoice always, pray continually," Paul writes in 1 Thessalonians. "Give thanks in all circumstances; for this is God's will for you in Christ Jesus" (5:16–18).

Though I now strive for a prayerful spirit always, on a day-to-day basis my prayer life varies. Some days are better than others when it comes to waking with a prayer on my lips. Sometimes I find myself so focused on making breakfast, getting my kids to school on time, and making sure everyone has clean clothes to wear and healthy food to eat that my morning greeting to God gets completely lost in all the harried action. And yet, in performing these acts with a prayerful spirit, my service to my family becomes my living prayer. In these ways we cultivate prayer *within* the harried action.

In an attempt to be mindful of the spirituality of the daily, I have prayers and quotes and Scripture written down and tacked up in places I'm sure to see them. Maybe then, for at least a moment, even in the midst of everyday tasks, I will find my center and I will remember a higher loving presence. One such reminder, the poem "Praying" by Mary Oliver, is written in permanent marker on the windowsill above my desk. Attractive design? Probably not. An in-your-face-reminder of God's love and my communion with him? Indeed. She says: "It doesn't have to be the blue iris, it could be weeds in a vacant lot, or a few small stones; just pay attention, then patch a few words together and don't try to make them elaborate, this isn't a contest, but a doorway into thanks, and a silence in which another voice may speak."[1]

These words have ultimately instructed my personal prayer life and given me comfort in a communal setting. They may also comfort those you're praying with. Often, my moms' group would take a moment for each woman to vocalize praises and prayer requests in a conversational style and then one member of our group would offer a collective prayer as we all bowed our heads and concentrated in silence. I was thrilled by the idea of communal prayer at the beginning or end of our Tuesday morning meetings, but I have to admit that I was terrified at the thought of praying aloud when my turn came.

Growing up as a Catholic, I was more accustomed to scripted prayers. I have said countless "Hail Marys" and "Our Fathers," both silently to myself and aloud in the presence of others. These prayers are purposeful and beautiful and comfortable to recite aloud in public, but in the case of our moms' group, I wanted to be able to pray more specifically for our time together and for the women sitting around me. This made me very nervous. Sometimes, as I mustered the courage to do so, it was hard to find the right words and, even though I loved and felt loved by the women around me, I still felt intimidated by an audience. Luckily, there are no "right" words. All we need to do is what Mary Oliver suggests, simply "patch a few" together. The act of engaging with God is enough. The gathering of the group itself is poetic; be assured that your prayers aren't required to be.

No matter how nervous it makes you or how tongue-tied you feel when sharing your intimate prayer life with others, there is no doubt that this brave act of praying together in community strengthens friendships. There is an intimacy that is established by allowing others into our prayer lives. And by allowing God to enter into our relationships and our collective endeavors, we grow in strength. James encourages us to engage in prayer with and for one another. "Confess your sins to each other and pray for each other so that you may be healed," he writes. "The prayer of a righteous person is powerful and effective" (5:16). When your group meets, no matter how anxious you are to start chatting, thank God for your time together and petition his presence.

In this way we follow the lead of the apostles, who prayed together constantly. The community of Jesus-followers written about in the Acts of the Apostles was faithful in prayer. We know that they prayed in communion with one another, before meals, and in their homes. Paul prays for the people he writes to, asking God to protect, strengthen, and guide.

As a group, you and your fellow moms might pray in many different ways and over time become more and more comfortable sharing this intimate act with one another. Communal prayers can be said out loud. Individuals can take turns leading prayers. You might write prayers and read them aloud. Perhaps you'll choose themes and meditate on them for the week. September prayers might focus on school-aged children. December prayers can center on the birth of Jesus and a season filled with grace and peace rather than harried shopping trips and too-long to-do lists. February prayers might focus on the politics of warmth. Eventually, the discipline of prayer will become something that you crave and enjoy. Even after our Wrigleyville moms' group moved apart and spread out all over the country, we continued to send prayer requests and praises via email. This practice continued to strengthen our relationships and impact our lives despite the distance.

As your group grows in relationship with one another and then begins to explore the idea of loving outwardly, prayer is essential. Your group will benefit by establishing a pattern of prayer regardless of how uncomfortable, forced, or awkward this might feel at first. Taking the time to pray with and for one another is a practice as crucial to your group as a runner carbo-loading and stretching before a marathon or a pianist warming up with scales before a performance.

Where might you begin? Anne Lamott makes the case for simplicity in her book about prayer called *Help, Thanks, Wow: The Three Essential Prayers.* "My three prayers," she writes, "are variations on Help, Thanks, Wow. That's all I ever need, besides the silence, the pain, and the pause sufficient for me to stop, close my eyes, and turn inward."[2]

Help us, God, as we adventure together as mothers with hearts full of love! Help us understand your purpose for us. Guide our Mama Bear instincts and help us to see the ways in which we can serve you and your people. Help us in our relationships and our endeavors.

Thank you, God, for our time together today. Thank you for the women in this group, for our life-giving bodies, for our sharp minds, and for our compassionate hearts. Thank you for our children and the relationships that they are building with one another.

We are floored by your generosity, God. We are in awe of your love and your blessings. Our children are clothed, fed, and entertained by the portions you've provided. We are rich in family. We are rich in friendship. We are amazed by your unmistakable and abundant blessings. Wow.

And then listen.

Silence yourselves for a moment and allow his love to resonate. You may actually benefit from a literal moment of silence while you are gathered together. Or this may come later, after the meeting wherever you might find quiet—perhaps while you're driving home or preparing the evening meal or at the gym. As humans we love to take the wheel and take control. Sometimes our own ideas, even those of good intentions, clutter our communication and we forget to listen to God's voice, which is part of the conversation whether invited or not. Sometimes Mama Bear projects or ideas never come to fruition, not because you lack the skills or the time or the passion, but simply because it's not the right time or not the right place. Taking the time to be still, to slow yourself down and *really* listen takes discipline. Make it your practice to carve out time to allow for the silence in which another voice may speak. Discuss with each other the moments when you're able to steal this time, not only sharing your strategy for making room for it in your day, but also what you learn when you do.

As you're thinking about the action that your group might take to serve each other and the world around you and as you're busy evaluating your next step, ask God to weigh in on the subject, listen for God's voice, and be faithful in allowing God to guide your actions. All the while, make room in your precious time together to pray. Sit with your sisters and patch together a few words, repeat scripted prayers, lift up praises and petitions with a spirit of wonder, a posture of humility, and an expectation of mercy, guidance, protection, and love.

NOTES

[1] Mary Oliver, "Praying," *Thirst* (Boston: Beacon Press, 2006).

[2] Anne Lamott, *Help, Thanks, Wow* (New York: RiverHead Books, 2012), 8.

CHAPTER SIX

Mamas on a Mission

Paradise lies at the feet of a mother.
—Muhammad

ama Bear is most powerful—most poised and awake to the world—when in the company of others. By now I would imagine you've sensed that when you seek friendship with other mothers and tackle tough questions together in an attempt to better understand compassion, your life will be rich in friendship, in love, and in action. The initial connection within your group of mamas may be your stage in life, your shared interests, and your common geography, but your bonds will travel beyond the surface as you strive to be an authentic community who seeks the way of Jesus. Leaning on each other, praying with and for one another, and ultimately deciding to channel your energy, anger, and desire to do good things in the world will transform your experience and your friendships. In his first epistle, John writes that our love should not be just words and talk. "It must be true love, which shows itself in action" (1 John 3:18 GNT).

Your Mama Bear wants action. Just as Hosea described an adoring and impassioned God as a mighty Mama Bear, so is your power and hunger.[1] She's ready to swing her fierce arms, break a righteous sweat, and exhibit her power in ways that bring healing to the world and great personal joy. Mama Bear is ready to rumble, and there are all sorts of things you can do as a group to make it easier for Mama Bear to unleash her passion. So let's get practical. By doing so, we'll clear a path for your group of Mama Bears and all of their ferocious intentions.

First and foremost, your relationships are worth hiring a babysitter for. A sitter is necessary for your formal meet-ups. If you're gathering at a park or someone's kitchen later on in the week for fun and further discussion then, by all means, include the kiddos. However, scheduling a group meeting once a week or once a month where you can be undistracted, with the children hanging out in a separate room with a trusted adult, is crucial for your Mama Bear relationships and soul. Split the tab for this precious, undistracted time together. Tap a member of your moms' posse with the gifts of organization and communication and support her as she uses her gifts to make it happen. It's a sacred stretch of time and your soul will soar while not having to worry about the needs of your offspring for a moment. A kind sitter (or two) to care for your children while you meet is a beautiful and necessary investment.

Just as you must practice loving acts of kindness toward one another and train yourselves to pray with and for one another, your meetings must be intentional as well. This doesn't mean that you need to trade the diaper bag for the professional woman bag and stick to a tightly scheduled agenda. It doesn't mean that you cannot meet over coffee and tea in someone's living room (while the kids play with the sitter outside!). But it does mean that you should come to the meeting prepared to work and grow. Bring discipline.

Bring your Bible, your book, or your study guide. Be intentional about the depth of your engagement. You may be tempted to discuss the "easier" and "safer" topics of life, but by being lazy about your conversation, you will prevent your experience from being as fulfilling as it could be. Your relationships will suffer and your own personal growth will be stunted. Remember, you are for growth.

Depending on your group dynamic, you may need to prepare discussion questions to keep you on track. If a study is being completed or a book is being read, you may want to invite one individual to lead the discussion and help guide the time. If you are in between books and studies, it's wise to plan your time in another creative, useful way. For instance, you could invite a "mentor" mom to come speak and answer questions about her experiences and relationship with God. You could organize a "Lunch with a Purpose," focusing the discussion on a specific topic or set of questions, something that my group of Wrigleyville moms did many times. If you're engaged in a project or are on the brink of jumping into one, the discussion should stay focused on the nuts and bolts. It's likely that the time you meet is precious . . . a breath of fresh air from the typical routine, subject matter, and train of thought. Cherish this time. Give thanks for it and use it for the kingdom.

Amid the thrill of friendship and the busyness of motherhood, it can be difficult to quiet your brain and focus your thoughts beyond the immediate needs of your offspring. Consider this: at any given moment, you are likely entertaining several different thoughts and planning a myriad of responses and actions. *The baby is hungry, no wait, I just fed the baby; the baby must be tired. The toddler could fall from there; the toddler needs to get down. The toddler won't do what I ask? Perhaps I can convince him with this distraction. Oh, the baby. Yes, the baby needs a nap.* (Please don't tell me that I'm the only whose brain functions in this manner.)

It is sometimes tough to escape this harried, distracted pattern of thinking. Seeing your friends for the first time in a week, there is a lot you'd like to share. You have stories to tell and questions to ask. Often when I walked into the moms' group meeting place, I felt a flurry of excitement and couldn't wait to chat it up with my friends. It's difficult to save these conversations for later and to suppress the urge to dive into any old conversation during the time allotted for your group meeting—a time meant for nurturing a different part of your brain.

Practically speaking, it is wise to **plan playdates and lunch dates and walks at the park beyond your official meeting**. During these more informal moments of friendship, we can hash over the incidentals of motherhood. (Car seat questions, adventures in potty training, the free-range parenting philosophy, whether or not to sign up for youth sports, for example). That way, there is plenty of time to cover all points of conversation and continue to strengthen each other and develop friendships.

In the simple words of Johnny Cash, when you meet together in a formal moms' group capacity, "Keep your eyes on Jesus."

Building a ministry from the ground up or steering an established ministry toward new pastures requires thoughtfulness and intentionality. Although your moms' group may feel very organic in its roots, a common direction is imperative in order to get the most out of your time together. This should be established early on in your group setting and revisited constantly. No matter how strong your friendships, in times of discord or distraction, these basic guidelines will help get the group back on track.

There are hundreds of books and resources available for small groups building a ministry. For a group of Mama Bears who are anxious to live and love out loud, the five basic steps that follow are the most essential as you establish yourselves as a group committed to fighting injustice with radical compassion.

Share your story of God's call to this group. Everyone has a unique story about how she arrived at motherhood, and it's typically one that we are happy to share with a captive audience. We enjoy hearing birth stories and the common experience of childbirth that can be so remarkably different than our own and yet so relatable. Sharing this, as well as the continued journey to the group, is an exercise in getting to know one another intimately. Showing that the women gathered are women who truly listen to each story establishes a basis of trust and gives everyone the confidence to offer their individual voice and perspective to the group. Sharing these stories is a great place to start your journey together.

Establish a vision statement. Your vision statement should tell the world about the ways in which you hope to change it. What do you want to see more of in your homes, your neighborhood, your country, or your world? Why is it that you have gathered? What do you hope to accomplish? After discussing the hopes and expectations that each person has for the group, write down a succinct statement that will guide the books you read, the studies you complete, the conversations you have, and the work you do. Each group will come up with its own unique statement of vision according to its members, but it might look something like this: "Our vision is to be a community of mothers who, bolstered by friendship and love of a common God, will take note of the injustice, inequality, and suffering around us and use our God-given gifts to pour our compassion into the world with creativity, resourcefulness, and great joy."

Establish a mission statement. Your mission statement will be a continuation of this vision. It answers the question: How on earth will we accomplish all of this? Start by discussing the nuts and bolts of your group meetings and consider what you can do with and for one another that will prepare your mission. Will you pray? Will you read the Bible? What about books? Again, every group will have its own mission statement, but yours might look like this: "We are a group of women committed to growing in our relationship with God and in our relationships with one another. We will strive to grow through prayer, study, conversation, and a commitment to community."

Together your statements will read something like this: "Our vision is to be a community of women who, bolstered by friendship and love of a common God, will take note of the injustice, inequality, and suffering around us and use our God-given gifts to pour our compassion into the world with creativity, resourcefulness, and great joy. We will accomplish this by growing in our relationship with God and with one another through prayer, study, conversation, and our commitment to our community, allowing this love and friendship to bolster our confidence to do good work in the world."

Create values. Your core values will help create meaningful meetings. What values must be present within each group meeting in order for your mission statement and vision statement to be fulfilled? How will you honor one another and the time you spend together? Knowing your group dynamic and the nature of your group, you will make a unique list of values that will hopefully be honored during your allotted group time each time you meet. You may start with basics such as respecting your time, committing to prayer, keeping conversation focused on the study or task at hand, valuing each group member's contribution, and actively listening to one another. The group's values should be written down and revisited along with your statements of mission and vision.

Sketch an outline. To whatever degree you are comfortable, sketch a flexible outline for the group. This may include a few months or an entire year. Discuss the things you'd like to focus on in an established block of time and commit to filling in the details.

For instance, do you have a book you'd like to read together? What will you do after the book is done? How many outreach projects do you hope to engage in this year? Will these be local or international or does it matter? These questions should be discussed and a flexible plan should be made.

Maybe you'll be lucky like I was and a Veronica will walk into your life and help get a moms' group going. Or a Tesi will invite you to a group that's already moving and shaking. Or perhaps you'll have been the one to organize your peers. Either way, your group will learn to take care of one another, pray together, and take the time to be an intentional example of Christ's love in action. You will learn to focus during your time together and reap the rewards. By being intentional about putting in the work, your Mama Bear will be well on her way to making her mark on your community.

"Give me six hours to chop down a tree, and I will spend the first four hours sharpening the axe," is a statement widely attributed to our sixteenth president, Abraham Lincoln. Just as we instruct our children to take their time, think things through, and practice as they endeavor to learn a new skill, we too must be patient and thoughtful in establishing or focusing our ministry. Taking care of the nuts and bolts of a blossoming ministry may not be as exciting as time spent discussing a book or as invigorating as seeing a project come together, but in doing so, the groundwork is laid for beautiful relationships and remarkable work. It's unlikely you'll be able to successfully channel the rage and power of a rumbling Mama Bear overnight—she's too powerful for that. It takes perseverance, a supportive network, and careful sharpening of, in this case, claws.

After considering the overarching values and expectations that will guide your group, your weekly interaction requires a similar thoughtfulness and discipline. Moms' meetings will be fun, but just as we give our children boundaries in which to experience the joy of the world, we can enjoy one another within the parameters of a meeting.

The mama with a business bent or a background in education will love the idea of setting meeting norms as you engage in energetic conversation and creative brainstorming. These norms may be similar to your group values, but more specific depending on the goals of the day. I bring them up here because although brainstorming and discussing dreams can be lively and joyful, it can also become divisive and demoralizing if we are not careful. Establishing meeting norms and discussion expectations will help keep your conversations productive and peaceful.

One step your moms' group can take before the meeting commences is to outline the expectations of your time together. This is especially useful if you are engaging in a Mama Bear brainstorming session and expectations should be made clear before the floodgates open and ideas begin to generate. You can personalize this to your unique group dynamic, but you may want to start with a few of the following basic brainstorming norms. For instance, in a healthy brainstorming session, participants will avoid immediately evaluating or debating the merits of each idea. Evaluation comes later; your immediate purpose is to generate as many ideas as possible. Assuming you value one another's voices and have already established a safe environment in which everyone feels free to participate in conversation, the ideas will flow freely and creatively. The grade-school adage holds true: there are no bad ideas in a brainstorming session. Also basic is that one mama should keep her eye on the time and another should take notes.

As you discuss how your group will channel Mama Bear's energy, welcome and embrace any and all ideas and avoid distracting side conversations. Though this might go without saying, energy will undoubtedly elevate during the dreaming and we may need help reining in conversation. Another important reminder for a group of passionate women who have formed meaningful relationships is to avoid lengthy backstories that might accompany ideas. Some external information is fine, but be sure that during these sessions, storytelling is minimal and the conversation stays on track.

Enjoy the powerful energy that is present as you meet to bounce ideas off of one another. In doing so, you'll catch a glimpse of the creativity of God in the ways in which each of you identify and approach the problems of the world. You'll likely be amazed by a mother's capacity for love, as well as the brilliance of the women you're surrounded by, as you strive for consensus. You'll continue to be amazed as these ideas take root. You'll start to feel the transformation. A group of intentional moms who gather for community, study, prayer, and perhaps a cup of coffee can quickly become part of a remarkable and much-needed solution in beautiful and surprising ways.

As you define your purpose as a group and begin to settle on a mission that everyone can be excited about, it's important that the group evaluates their collective talents. As discussed previously, we are all created different and embody different strengths and talents that can be used to further God's kingdom here on earth. Don't underestimate your own influence. When we work collectively, we have the very real opportunity to avoid the tasks that we simply don't enjoy or do not have a propensity for and instead focus on the things we are good at and the things that bring us joy.

Our gifts will reveal themselves in the beginning, and from the start each mama should contribute in a way that comes naturally to her. This is true in the execution of the plan for service, but it should also play out in the initial planning stages. So ask yourself again when considering your Mama Bear work, where do her strengths lie? What would she enjoy? Where does she best fit in each step of service?

It is likely that you have a dreamer in your group. This person can lead your brainstorm sessions. Follow her lead. She will bring all kinds of creative ideas and enthusiasm as you try to define your goal or your project.

It is also likely that someone among you is a list-making mama; maybe you'll even have a spreadsheet-making mama. Let her take notes and make charts to her heart's content. Even though it's not everyone's cup of tea, there are people in this world who can feel the love of God in the face of an Excel document or Google Sheet.

Someone will be task oriented; enlist her to help rein in the conversation if things start to meander. (They will.)

Some of us are born to encourage and support. This role is crucial in a group, and your encourager should be allowed to do so to her heart's content.

From the beginning, each mama should boldly jump in with her God-given gifts. She will find great joy in her contribution and the group will see great worth in her talents.

In fact, we need everyone to bring her own gifts to the table. Just as I rely on mama friends to fill me in on parenting strategies and diaper deals, I can rely on them to do the tasks I dread when endeavoring to begin a project. We each come to the table with unique strengths. I am a dreamer and an idea generator. I sit on the edge of my seat during good brainstorming sessions. But I lack organization and follow-through. Without the gifts, talents, and help of others, my ideas are useless.

> The way God designed our bodies is a model for under-
> standing our lives together as a church: every part
> dependent on every other part, the parts we mention
> and the parts we don't, the parts we see and the parts we

don't. If one part hurts, every other part is involved in the hurt, and in the healing. If one part flourishes, every other part enters into the exuberance. (1 Cor. 12:25–26 *The Message*)

It's important for your moms' group to assess your talents while you think of possibilities. Respect the talents and dreams of your fellow mamas and encourage everyone to use her gifts as part of a team.

One blustery afternoon, I took a quick peek at Facebook while my two-year-old stacked blocks at the corner of the couch and my four-year-old took my order for the "diner" he was running out of our kitchen. As I scrolled through pictures and proclamations, I noticed my friend Jenny's status enthusiastically announcing that she and her missional moms' group were selling sugar cookies for Valentine's Day and giving the proceeds to an organization close to her heart. Though I hadn't seen Jenny in several years, her words made perfect sense to me. Jenny was a friend from college and I fondly remembered the "wine and cheese" nights that she would host in her small apartment. A dozen or so girlfriends would gather after finals to eat delicious appetizers and drink wine while catching up. I knew Jenny and her large Italian family loved food and loved to cook, and here she was—a decade later—putting her interest and passion to work to raise money to combat human trafficking.

We can all follow Jenny and her group's lead. Just don't expect everyone to bake. Some of us much prefer purchasing cookies from the bakery or the grocery store and aren't cut out for extended time in the kitchen. After discovering the things that make each of us move, embrace every individual's unique interests and talents and make the cause fit them. Let the graphic design mama design attractive labeling. Tap your marketing mama to promote the product and your PR mama to write the press release. Volunteer to make the margaritas while you let the bakers bake. Bare your talent in the way that feels like a soul-enriching gift rather than another chore that you're obligated to do. God rests in these moments. Your great joy becomes actionable in his kingdom.

Identifying these gifts and celebrating them with one another is part of the fun. One summer, years after completing the *Networking* study referenced earlier, our moms' group revisited the idea of identifying where our talents lie by completing a personality test. As we were sitting around the picnic table drinking wine and eating grilled veggies and chicken, we took turns discussing each woman's outcome. What began as a fun and funny activity—akin to the "love predictor" test in a magazine like *Cosmo*—turned into a rather beautiful moment of love and charity. Not only were we interested in our own personal score, we were curious to see how others were described. As results were read aloud, there were comments like: "Oh, I love that about you, Sarah!" and "Yes! Lisa, I can totally see that trait in the way you treat your daughter!" Things like: "Lindsay, you *are* good at that!"

We took the time to identify individual strengths and then to celebrate the one who possessed them. The conversation was positive and soul enriching. It reinforced our love and respect for one another and made for uplifting dinnertime conversation. We praised one another and challenged one another as good friends and as dynamic citizens of the world.

Be generous to one another and be generous with your life. Give your love away. I love the song lyric written by my talented friend Andy: "Give it all away while you're here. Leave nothing but love behind."[2] Use your talents and your true joy to serve others. In doing so, you will find fulfillment and tap into a part of your brain that perhaps you tend to neglect during the everyday business of child-rearing and the tasks of family life. Working toward a common goal will strengthen your friendships. You will learn to take risks and to rely on one another and on God. The Mama

Bear lurking inside will use your group momentum and your individual talents and blessings, and she will make sure others benefit from your generosity, in ways large and small. When your group is carefully planned and prayerfully cultivated, everyone wins by bearing witness to these relationships. It's the perfect marriage between love and more love.

NOTES

[1] Hosea 13:8 says, "Like a bear robbed of her cubs, I will attack them and rip them open." Whoa! Mama Bear is also mentioned in 2 Samuel 17:8: "You know your father and his men; they are fighters, and as fierce as a wild bear robbed of her cubs."

[2] Andrew Landers and Mainstreet Struggleville, www.mainstreetstruggleville .com.

PART THREE

The thought of seeing one of the world's great predator species in the wild is a magical idea for many people. But soon you'll be praying that you don't when you're alone and lost in the mountains. That cuddly toy image of a bear will evaporate very quickly in grizzly bear country.

—Bear Grylls, *Man vs. Wild*

CHAPTER SEVEN

Supermom Must Die

I probably should have mentioned this earlier. I'm poison.
—Poison Ivy to Mr. Freeze, *Batman and Robin* (1997)

Once, while deep in the throes of a midmorning playdate, a few fellow moms and I bravely challenged one another to make a list of the "super" characteristics that we were trying to embody. We called it the "Supermom List" and spent a few days reflecting on the ways in which we were vainly trying to fit into mom-sized superhero costumes. This list was our version of the perfect mother and woman—the person we hoped others saw when they laid eyes on us. It was a dangerous idea and a treacherous mission.

Allow me to introduce my very own, very frightening, version of Supermom:

1. Supermom cooks entirely healthy, balanced, organic meals for her family five days a week. Supermom whips these dishes up from scratch with ingredients found in her well-stocked pantry and her kitchen garden. She is creative and confident in the kitchen!

2. Supermom works outside the home at least twenty hours each week without ever needing to hire a babysitter! She is constantly inspired and disciplined. Because she doesn't require much sleep, she gets up before her children and uses early morning light to accomplish great things.

3. Supermom loves to exercise. She takes action-packed trips to her gym regularly and enthusiastically. Oh! You should see her on the treadmill! She pushes herself to new limits every single day.

4. Supermom never loses patience. Her voice is calm and even at all times. She believes every moment with her children is precious and ripe with teaching potential. She is never too tired to read another story and, with children in tow, she is never running too late to stop and inspect a rock, flower, or interesting crack on the sidewalk. But don't think for a second that Supermom is a pushover. This woman is firm and fair. Supermom is an unwavering, mighty master of discipline.

5. Supermom reads every single issue of the *New Yorker*, hot off the press and in its entirety. She laughs uproariously at each cartoon and is able to recall each article in astonishing detail in conversation. She is witty, she is engrossing, she is brilliant!

6. Supermom is super cute. She is fashionable to boot and her look is effortless, giving off the appearance of uncultivated perfection. She's got a sixth sense for style and wears age-appropriate trends that capture the spunk of youth and the elegance of womanhood. Only sustainably harvested cotton touches her skin and her roots always match the rest of her perfectly coiffed and highlighted hair.

7. Supermom is artistic and able. When her son comes home with a hole in his jeans, she mends it without blinking. Did you say someone needs an original Halloween costume with only a moment's notice? No problem, she says, as she sits down at the sewing machine. Supermom suppresses the urge to curse as she sews or drink heavily as she finishes a particularly challenging project at the very last minute. She is inventive, she is creative, and her fine-motor skills dazzle!

8. Supermom simultaneously balances love and devotion to her children with love and devotion to her partner. When they reunite at the end of each day she is never tired or cranky or demanding. She creates a restful home with an atmosphere of love and an ambience of peace and tranquility (regardless of the hundreds of Legos littering the floor and the likely screaming toddler with the blueberry-stained face in the corner). Supermom moonlights as Superwife.

9. Supermom is a super friend. She makes time for all of her girlfriends and is at their beck and call. She is known for her problem-solving skills and her empathy. She never misses a birthday and always sends thoughtful (handmade with love, of course!) gifts on time.

10. Supermom is a volunteer extraordinaire. If you're in a bind, call on Supermom to get the job done. She'll bake, she'll clean, she'll even drive the bus! There is no fundraising project too big, no errand too small for this good-hearted heroine.

This is the very long list that I created. I had compiled a woman with ridiculously amazing, out-of-this-world traits. A heroic woman who I thought I should be more like. A woman so talented, intelligent, and incredible that had I met her on the street, I'm not sure I would even like her.

Supermom caused a problem for me because when I stood next to her, the real me didn't stand a chance. The real me paled in comparison and seemed hopelessly inadequate next to the armor of the woman I had created in my mind. Though my ideals were mostly well-intentioned, they proved to be detrimental in that they led to feelings of failure and ineptitude.

Where did I get this idea? Was I really telling myself that this is who God had made me to be? Supermom had a way of making me feel inadequate when I was unable to live up to her magnificence in my daily life. Why had I invited this idea of a supermom in, and why was I letting her stay?

Ultimately, seeing this person spelled out in front of me was freeing. The sheer length of my list was enough to make me realize that I was trying to accomplish the humanly impossible in a single day. It made my head spin. How would I ever have time to love my children or notice the world around me if I were trying to live up to all of the amped-up elements of this superwoman? Supermom may look good on paper, but upon closer look, she had no substance. She was spread too thin, and in her quest for perfection, she was missing out on many of the simple, meaningful moments of life. Supermom needed some focus. She needed a clearer mission. She needed to be brought down a notch or two.

The women in my moms' group and I discussed this notion of perfection and how by constantly measuring ourselves against these unrealistic ideals, we were missing out on our true selves and forgetting to delight in who God made us to be. God speaks to Jesus after he is baptized by John in the Jordan and says, "This is my Son, whom I love; with him I am well pleased" (Matt. 3:17). This statement is for each of us as well. Stripped down and soaking wet, with unruly hair and smudged eyeliner, we are looked at by God, who says, "You are my daughter, whom I love; with you I am well pleased." We don't need the cape.

Since I took the time to pinpoint the out-of-this-world qualities of this woman with my mom friends, I have been at work to eliminate my nemesis, the Supermom. I no longer allow myself to feel guilty if I serve my family a frozen pizza on a Thursday night. I no longer beat myself up over letting magazines and newspapers pile up only half read. I am no longer disappointed in myself if I go to the gym only for an easy stationary bike ride and a long shower, or if I don't go to the gym at all. There are stretches of time that I wear the same outfit day after day. I allow my husband to see the real me at the end of the day, and as flustered as I sometimes am, I believe we're both happier because of it. All of this enables a colossal, soul-cleansing sigh of relief.

Taking off our superhero mask benefits not only ourselves but those around us as well. After my girlfriends and I started to discuss our Supermoms, we became more real with one another. Shedding the cape made me more authentic to those I was in relationship with. For instance, I realized (and my friends seemed to as well) that if I wanted to spend the morning hanging out with friends, I needed to spend less time worrying about having the "right" type of snacks for the moms and kiddos (all organic, plenty of veggies, perfect lattes) and invite them over anyway. That doesn't mean that I cannot treat my guests with great love and hospitality, but striving for perfection can be paralyzing. Too often, if I didn't feel like I could achieve the "perfect" morning playdate, I would skip it altogether. I don't want to miss out on moments of friendship and community because I am afraid of exposing the chinks in my armor. I don't want to suffer at the hands of Supermom.

My girlfriends and I were not alone. Erma Bombeck, a twentieth-century American writer, faces her "super" in a column entitled,

"If I Had My Life to Live Over Again." Her words are raw and full of regret:

> I would have invited friends over to dinner even if the
> carpet was stained and the sofa faded. I would have sat
> on the lawn with my children and not worried about
> grass stains. I would never have bought anything just
> because it was practical, wouldn't show soil or was guar-
> anteed to last a lifetime. When my child kissed me
> impetuously, I would never have said, "Later. Now get
> washed up for dinner." There would have been more I
> love yous, more I'm sorrys, but mostly, given another
> shot at life, I would seize every minute, look at it and
> really see it, live it, and never give it back.[1]

I think it's safe to say that Bombeck, who was born in 1927, struggled with her own version of Supermom. Reading her words fills
me with sorrow, but I am grateful she took a moment to use her
experience to instruct a new generation of readers. I hear the sadness and regret that live in these words and feel tense seeing the
declarations in ink. I feel this because I understand exactly what
she is saying and have lived it myself.

I have worried about grass stains. I have walked through periods of life too quickly—not pausing to pay due attention to God's
abundant blessings because I was too worried about what I was
wearing or whether or not the living room had been vacuumed
or because I was speeding through my to-do list. There have been
periods of solitude and loneliness strictly because I was too worried
about whether or not what I had to offer was organic, local, and
homemade. Unless I engage the battle with Supermom, I feel inadequate and therefore isolated. Don't worry about baking, Bombeck
would tell me: purchase a dessert from the market (or skip dessert
altogether) and call your friends.

She may look very different for all of us, but I truly believe most mothers have a version of Supermom lurking on the sidelines. And most of us, I think, are anxious to shed our capes and reveal our true selves to our friends and families, however cracked and flawed we think we may be. This is what Shauna Niequist craves as she writes about the chains of perfection in her memoir *Bittersweet*:

> We slip into believing that it's better to strive for perfection than to accept and offer one another grace. . . . What I need as a mother is grace. God's grace, that allows me to fail and try again, that allows me to ask for help when I don't have the wisdom or patience I need, that reminds me we're not alone in this, and that God loves my son even more than I do. And grace from other mothers. I need grace and truth-telling camaraderie from other moms. I need us to tell the truth about how hard it is, and I need us to help each other, instead of hiding behind the pretense and pressure of perfection.[2]

When we let ourselves off the hook for all of our imperfection, we let those around us off the hook as well. We love for who we are, not who we think we should be. God lends us this grace by promising his love to us regardless. We need to lend the same grace to ourselves and to one another. "You are my daughter, and with you I am well pleased."

Because my community of women tackled Supermom, I have become less afraid of admitting my shortcomings to my friends. In fact, I think we tend to respect one another when we are honest and humble much more than we do when we keep the facade 100 percent "put together" and lead a dangerous double life. I recently sat down at a Little League game with my friend Dana. When she asked how I was doing, I decided to tell her the truth. The morning had not gone well. I was so frustrated with my children and so overwhelmed by life that I lost my cool, angrily pushed a kitchen chair to the floor, and stomped out of the room in a rage. (A glimpse of Mama Bear's power, to be sure. I pushed a chair over!) Rather than responding by saying "fine" and moving on with the conversation, I was honest with Dana, who has been my friend for years. She didn't judge me or tell me I was a bad mom. Instead, she comforted me with words of understanding and grace. With the conversation came a release of guilt as well as a renewed understanding that parenting is hard and that I'm not alone. Coming face-to-face with our friends and opening up with truth and vulnerability enables us to enjoy true fellowship with one another.

It was shortly after I made the obnoxious superhero list and attempted to slay my archnemesis that I began to notice something about the stripped-down me and the response I managed to elicit. One late afternoon, my then-three-year-old Oliver was red-cheeked and tired from fighting the imaginary bad guys who had apparently invaded our living room, when he rushed into the kitchen where I was making dinner. (I'll be honest: part of this dinner may have come from a box. Do I feel bad about this? Not really.)

"Mommy Power Ranger?" he panted. "Can you get me a glass of water?" It was a simple request, though epic to him.

I stared down at Oliver, who was sporting his well-worn Spiderman costume, craning his neck to meet my eyes. His body was quite literally too small to reach the sink, let alone the cupboard where the glasses are stored.

"Of course," I said, and in one quick motion I grabbed a cup, filled it up with cold water, and put it in his upstretched hand. He drank greedily, set the cup on the table, and ran out of the room, yelling something about a Ninja Turtle.

In this moment with my son, I realized that I have nothing to fear. I may shed the cape, but I will still impress the ones that matter. In the eyes of the little people that I parent and those who love me, I'm capable of amazing feats. Pulling a cup down from the cupboard and doing the small favor of filling it up with water is only the beginning.

You, too, are capable of such amazement. To those who look to you for love, favor, and guidance, your actions are heroic, whether the world would classify them that way or not. It's when we silence the negative self-talk and cast off the high expectations that we so often place on ourselves that we can begin to appreciate just how spectacular we are within our tiny corner of the world.

This, I believe, is the most wonderful realization of all—one that I have thought of often as I am trying to put back on my too-tight Supermom costume and live up to the list. I think of the wonder in my child's eyes as I spread peanut butter on his bread or grab a baseball that has soared out of his reach. I think of my daughter's smile when I show up at her classroom in school. She doesn't care what I'm wearing or what snack I brought. Her mom showed up and it's enough to make her day. It's simple servanthood; it's doing small things with great love. I see the adoring expression in my child's eyes, and I am reminded that giving my best self (my true self, not my hyped-up, superself) is exactly what I am made to do— nothing more, nothing less.

And even then—especially then—God will use you to bring his light to the world. You *are* capable of amazing feats, and it's not just your children who believe this to be true. God believes you're capable as well. Otherwise, why would he have tasked us with loving radically and serving extravagantly and bringing heaven to earth? God trusts us, imperfect and unimpressive as we are, to bring glory in both big and little ways here in the land of the living. This is the self that needs to show up to your moms' group meetings each week. This is the authenticity that will eventually make positive change in the world.

You don't have to attend much Sunday school or listen to many sermons to realize that, over and over again, God uses the little guy to bring his glory to earth. He doesn't seek the perfectly coiffed or the expert multitasker to perform miracles. It was young, red-haired David, bolstered by confidence in God, who slayed the giant. It was Mary, an unwed teenage mother, who provided the holy vessel for the man who shook the world. A scared and intimidated Moses did heroic things. And remember the time God spoke through a donkey?[3] Clearly, awe-inspiring things are accomplished through the not-so-super among us.

It would seem that a righteous idea of "super" or "hero" is much different than what our current culture declares it to be. Though we are constantly bombarded by external messages exalting a certain standard of life—the "right" way to look and act and make your way through the world—God holds no such pretenses. And yet we make the mistake of comparing ourselves to the images we see and the words we read and of measuring ourselves by the standards of social media. Trying to live up to these ideas and images is exhausting. Even the most well-cultivated wardrobe will only last for a season. Balsam fir draped on the banister during the holidays will be replaced next year by boxwood. As we chase this month's "it" list, next month's issue hits the newsstands, and we feel like we have to catch up once again. It is likely that we don't have the time, energy, or money to live up to the flawless social feeds and media messages. And even if we do, we may not find it all that fulfilling.

I probably don't have to remind you of the popular notion that a woman is capable of "having it all." Typically, "having it all" refers to a work-life balance and, typically, the articles, essays, and books draw the same conclusion: if you manage to "have it all," you'll be too harried and exhausted to enjoy it. If you don't "have it all," you'll never be satisfied and always feel like you're missing out on something.

Many women struggle with this every day, and the very essence of the idea is what fuels the myth of the Supermom. This bears repeating: it's a myth. I haven't come across anyone who "has it all" and is as happy as the world would have us think. If you think you know a real-life, living and breathing Supermom, sit down and talk to her. Really talk to her. Ask her questions and listen closely. You'll soon find that everyone struggles with something. There are always sacrifices being made.

More and more, I'm casting aside the idealization (or existence) of balance, and instead embracing a life full of changing seasons and varying paces. At any given time, it's more productive and compelling to focus on "having it"—the "it" being God's purpose for you—rather than "having it all." Paul writes in Philippians 3:15: "Let's keep focused on that goal, those of us who want everything God has for us" (*The Message*). I am convinced that God would not be impressed by my ability to recount at dinner parties articles I've read in astonishing detail. He would rather I not worry so much about what to wear, and he certainly doesn't care what kind of car I drive. Does Jesus encourage us to be in community with friends? Yes. Does he care what I'm wearing when we gather? No.

Shedding the cape is important because it helps us to prioritize and frees us to become the most faithful version of ourselves at this point in our lives. If you are reading this book, it is likely that you have come to motherhood in one way or another. It's likely you take this role very seriously and are very much invested in being the best mother you can be to your children. Also likely is that you're trying to maintain a bit of your identity as you navigate parenthood. This is a quest that takes constant reevaluating and readjusting in order to fully embrace the enormous role with which you have been tasked, while maintaining a sense of self in the process. It takes heartfelt conversation with yourself and those who love you. It requires honesty with ourselves and with others.

Such things are important to wade through because once we evaluate our priorities and reposition ourselves as caretakers to another person in addition to being vibrant individuals, we can shape the healthy version of ourselves. When we do this, we not only free ourselves to be the amazing women we were created to be in this moment in time, but we can look forward to new growth and personal development. Before my first son was born, I had no idea that I was physically capable of waking every three hours every single night for months on end and still being able to put one foot in front of the other during the day. I love sleep and honestly didn't think I could survive on so little. Becoming a mother taught me otherwise. I used to think that I needed to shampoo every single day in order to show myself to the world and be deemed respectable. Who knew that doing so only a once a week actually feels healthier? I have felt the rumble of a Mama Bear and my anger has penetrated more deeply than I could have ever imagined. I had no idea that I could love so fiercely. It wasn't until a little person started calling me "mama" that I was awakened to these truths and began to allow them to coexist with the woman I had always been.

Though there are challenges in navigating this new terrain, doing so broadens our horizons and allows for extreme personal growth. Not only do our little bundles of babe teach us practical life lessons (the physical miracles of childbirth and breast-feeding, for starters), they also bring a burst of new energy, new levels of compassion, and a new depth of feeling and understanding. The whole experience is a tremendous catalyst for remarkable personal growth.

As we embrace our new role in life, we find that it often comes with a new rhythm, a new circle of influence, and a new radar on the world. When we are grounded in the love of God and hence motivated by this love, we can use this new position in life (no matter what it is) and further his kingdom. But in order for this to be fully realized, we must first determine what it is that truly matters to us and guard our priorities closely.

More often than not, the things we are tempted or feel pressure to chase conflict with what is realistic for our family and the ways in which God might intend to guide our hearts. Like handing a glass of water to a teeny-tiny sidekick when he can't reach the sink, our most important acts of love may not be glossy or glamorous, and they will likely begin close to home. And though home may not seem as invigorating as a job downtown and an expense account, with a healthy perspective we can find it enthralling. Ideally, we would train ourselves to go through our daily lives alert to the everyday happenings in our homes. We would be in the practice of recognizing the blessings and noticing the injustice. If this is not something that you typically think about as you journey through your day, then this is the perfect time to practice.

With your moms' group in mind, prepare yourself by examining your everyday posture. Be mindful of the way you react to the world. Consider the challenges, frustrations, mysteries, and joys of each day. Motherhood does not come with the trappings of a rock star. It takes some internal work and self-reflection to banish the idea that we should *be more* and that life should *offer more*. Regardless of how you best arrive there (it may take a disciplined practice of intentional journaling, honest conversation, prayer, or meditation), endeavor to identify and fully understand the joys that are yours to have—the blessings of a new schedule, a comfortable pair of flats, and naptime. By focusing on the true desires of your heart, you can train yourself to believe that the moment is enough and that each breath is exactly as it should be. As is written in Proverbs, "Give me your heart . . . and keep your eyes fixed on my ways" (23:26 isv).

Author Ann Voskamp works to find the magnificent in the everyday in her book *One Thousand Gifts: A Dare to Live Fully Right Where You Are* and ultimately tries to answer a question that we might all ask ourselves: "How do you open the eyes to see how to take the daily, domestic workday vortex and invert it into the dome of an everyday cathedral?" This question became urgent for Voskamp, and she developed a practice for growth that becomes compulsive. What is holy in your everyday, ordinary life as it is right now? What is remarkable about the seemingly mundane life you lead? How do you find God in your everyday existence? Voskamp begins with a gratitude journal in which she records one thousand everyday blessings. She records things like paper bag puppet shows and a whistling teakettle and finds that the practice leads her to more thankfulness, more joy, and a more fulfilling communion with the world.[4]

Recently, I felt ready to make another list, this time a list like Voskamp's. I have found that this list is much more forgiving and full of hope than the one I penned years ago while combating my version of Supermom with my mom friends. However, had I not first recognized Supermom and acknowledged her prowess in my life, I am not sure I would have been able to appreciate the unremarkable (by worldly standards) moments of my everyday minutiae that I recently put down on paper. The way our leaded glass windows cast dozens of small rainbows over our living room floor on sunny mornings. The loud, unsteady drumbeat played with unrelenting passion by my son on a snare. The adorable curl of my daughter's hair. The perfect tomato sliced onto a piece of bread slathered with mayonnaise and eaten at the kitchen table while our daughter naps and our boys are safe at school. These are the everyday miracles on my list. There is nothing seemingly "super" about any of these things, yet they are the dome of my cathedral. This running list of everyday joys helps me to more fully grasp God's presence in the ins and outs of my daily life. If this inner work is something that your moms' group navigates together, I trust that knowing this and pausing to recognize God's love and care in your life will ultimately propel you into becoming the change agents of this world.

This sort of personal self-reflection will benefit you as an individual and your moms' group as a whole. When we take the time to know ourselves, we can share ourselves more fully. When you gather with the women in your moms' group, bring your real self, with all your questions, and all your flaws. Do not invite Supermom to the party, the playdate, or the weekly meeting. In fact, it may be necessary to use the strength of your community to squash her unrelenting spirit. Identify Supermom with the support of one another. Write about her. Talk about her. Put her in her place. Don't let her get in the way of Micah's command to act justly, love mercy, and *walk humbly* with God (6:8).

If Supermom shows up (and chances are that she *will* show up), tell her to go back to her lair. Slowly extinguish her light from your life. Free yourself from her impulse toward perfection and her need for approval, and make room for the everyday miracles of the life God has given you. It's imperative. In order for you to channel your Mama Bear and for your moms' group to move forward and rattle the world, you've got to make room for the authentic and the good.

Supermom must die.

NOTES

[1] Erma Bombeck, "If I Had My Life to Live Over Again," At Wits End, December 2, 1979.

[2] Shauna Niequist, *Bittersweet* (Grand Rapids: Zondervan, 2013), 114.

[3] Numbers 22:26–33.

[4] Ann Voskamp, *One Thousand Gifts* (Grand Rapids: Zondervan, 2010).

CHAPTER EIGHT

Simple Is the New Super

Live simply, so others may simply live.
—Mother Teresa

I am pleased to tell you that Supermom has begun to slink into the shadows over the last half dozen or so years. It's not that she didn't put up a good fight. She did. But she now hides in a dusty closet and rarely tries to sneak out. It has been a slow eradication, buoyed by a community of friends, counseling, and regular meditation, and the mood and tempo of my life have shifted noticeably. With the defeat of this souped-up "heroine," I've found that I'm living a much more authentic version of myself. Allow me to tell you about the new me.

The new me loves lounging on the couch on Saturday mornings, covered with newspaper and sipping coffee at leisure. Little satisfies me more than sitting stationary on the floor for great lengths of time, watching my two sons perform magic tricks or hassle the dog. The new me makes time to visit coffee shops with a simple agenda of staring out windows, daydreaming, and ignoring anything that happens to be written in my planner. I spent last summer on our front porch comfortably nestled into a wicker settee, drinking iced tea and watching my daughter play in front of me with a bucket of water and a batch of plastic dinosaurs. The new me understands Walt Whitman when he writes in *Song of Myself*, "I loaf and invite my soul."

Supermom has left the building.

One might think this ability to happily do nothing would alter my ability to maintain relationships. One might even pity my poor family. But rest assured, our house is (mostly) clean, our children fed, and I have a few friends in my contact list to my credit. However, on my best days, I try not to break a sweat.

Over time I have slowly shed my insecurities that this lackadaisical attitude might inhibit the chances of my offspring socializing successfully or someday getting into a top-notch college. In fact, I have actually come to believe that this posture of nothingness is my best, most productive parenting strategy. My children and I stay at home whenever possible to paint, cook, or sort clothes from the dryer. A walk to the park, if we are feeling ambitious, suits us fine. We dance in the dining room to our favorite tunes, call it "Music and Movement with Mama," and consider it a private lesson that we don't have to change out of our pajamas for. All four of us love "unstructured free time," an important-sounding name for "You Do Your Thing and Mommy Will Watch from the Couch."

It's actually during these moments that Mama Bear is nourished and her rumblings recognized and explored under the surface. This allows the important inner work to take place—the soul is fed by quiet and predictability. It's during these moments that Mama Bear is primed and prepared to be set free.

It has been years since my mom friends and I first discussed our "super" and began the quest to banish the pesky nemesis. Part of the struggle has been getting over the idea that busyness equates success, as it does in many realms of American life. And to be honest, it still takes great effort to suppress the urge to run ragged trying to accomplish and acquire. At one point, in fact, I began feeling a bit insecure about my current posture. Supermom had snuck out of hiding and was on the brink of signing my kids up for every activity under the sun, all the while seriously fretting over the day's outfit. I needed sage advice and I looked to a fellow mother with more credentials than I for reassurance. I picked up the phone and sought advice from a psychologist, yoga instructor, and mother of two. In my moment of need, she answered the phone. Was that the clink of iced tea I heard in the background?

"Overstimulation is a problem in our culture. And honestly, kids are better than any of us at just being," Dr. Betsy Rippentrop told me calmly as I lamented my concerns. "What we try to impose on [our children] are all of these activities and things to do and places to be instead of allowing them to be present and be a kid. We're breeding the problem that's inherent as adults: we go all of the time, we never slow down, we never give ourselves breaks." There are days when I need this reinforcement as I mother my children and try to do what is best for our family. Often, there is a nagging feeling that what we're doing is just not quite enough . . . that perhaps we should have signed up for fall soccer and I that I should definitely learn to sew.

There is, of course, nothing wrong with being involved in activities that we enjoy. But I do believe that we can all benefit from staying quiet a bit more often. I keep reading about the "Secular Sabbath"—a day where smartphones are silenced, iPads kept out of sight, and social media left unchecked. Instead, we move about the day undistracted and completely immersed in the minutiae of every precious moment. These days of uninterrupted relaxation can inspire both a healthy sigh of relief and some of our best thinking. The wise Betsy says of a Sabbath experience, "It's an important step in trying to quiet down your life and your mind so that you can start to look inside yourself."

Quiet down your life. "Be still before the LORD," says the psalmist in Psalm 37. "Wait patiently for him." These are the moments when we've turned off the static and are open to God's love. We have time to notice the blessings and feel the divine in our lives.

A truth-telling friend recently reminded me of the moment when Jesus says to Peter, "You are a stumbling block to me; you do not have in mind the concerns of God, but merely human concerns" (Matt. 16:23). This is the kind of reminder I need when I get caught up in the daily, worldly challenges and forget about the grand scheme. It's words like these from Scripture and from friends that I respect that help quiet the "super" impulses.

So far my idle attitude hasn't caused many setbacks for those I love. Despite their short résumés, my children all enjoyed early education at a good preschool, and the neighborhood public school has no choice but to accept us for who we are: laid-back homebodies with, I believe, a bit more imagination than we might otherwise have developed. (According to some, all that "unstructured free time" is supposed to do wonders for a kid's creativity.)[1]

And when I am feeling insecure, I think of Betsy and how, much to my delight, she actually encourages me to slow down even more by taking a step toward formal meditation practice. "To really know lasting happiness and find contentment in your life," she says, "you have to look inside. There are formal practices that have been around for thousands of years that show us the way to know ourselves. Starting a formal meditation program or trying some yoga is important for people's development and their evolution as a human being." God bless her for her understanding, I think, before resuming my position on the couch.

Meditation is something that Christians have been practicing for thousands of years. It is an art of centering oneself and allowing space for God to enter. Jesus says in his Sermon on the Mount that you should find quiet and then "just be there as simply and honestly as you can manage. The focus will shift from you to God, and you will begin to sense his grace" (Matt. 6:6 *The Message*). Knowing this, something that once seemed very time-consuming, intimidating, and flat-out boring now appears to be something I might be able to manage.[2] Even when Jesus was in the full swing of his ministry, we see him retreating in prayer over and over again.

In the book *Celebration of Discipline*, Richard J. Foster writes about twelve pathways to spiritual growth and includes meditation as an important inward discipline. "What happens in meditation is that we create the emotional and spiritual space which allows Christ to construct an inner sanctuary in the heart."[3]

As a mother, it may seem difficult to imagine finding time to devote to such practice; however, we might find that when we ease into a slower lifestyle, a meditative spirit prevails. Foster seems to understand current constraints and reassures his reader that there is no one way to go about meditating. He claims that the first step is to simply slow down and make room for a conversation with God. He cautions that "if we are constantly being swept off our feet with frantic activity, we will be unable to be attentive at the moment of inward silence. A mind that is harassed and fragmented by external affairs is hardly prepared for meditation."[4]

Remembering this, I feel vindicated in (or at least less guilty about) my quest toward simplicity. The days when we are not harried or running from one place to another are the days that I am most open to the way God is moving in my life. I notice the small moments of grace and have time to acknowledge and be thankful for them. A sense of peace is more likely to fall upon our household when we are not rushing to get somewhere. During these times I speak more kindly to my children. I look them in the eye and really listen to what they have to say. It is when we are all crammed into our teeny-tiny pantry/back entryway trying to find shoes, coats, hats, and the proper equipment for wherever it is that we are going that I am most likely to lose my temper and show them my ugliness.

I have friends who manage this pace of life—this slower, intentional way of living—much better than I do. When I go to Michelle's house, for instance, there are candles burning and soft music playing. It is an oasis of calm, and the feeling has a direct impact on the way our children interact and the way we all treat one another. She begins each day with a period of quiet time and endeavors to take that peace with her as she moves about her day.

Even if this sounds lovely to you (it will undoubtedly sound strange to others), it is still sometimes difficult to accept this quest toward simplicity because so often we are led to believe that children will fall behind or be unable to reach their full potential if we deny seemingly important early childhood educational opportunities. I know plenty of moms who make sure their children participate in dance class, acting class, piano lessons, swim team, and soccer club. These mothers possess out-of-this-world organizational skills and make this schedule work for their family. They are good mothers and good people. But I don't see them often. They are very, very busy.

Some of these moms are innately social beings, have a high tolerance for activity, and actually thrive within their tight schedule. There are also moms who find that they struggle greatly with this pace and long to be set free. They want to do more and be more for their children, but they are left feeling harried, hurried, and wading in the pile of Happy Meal containers piled up in their minivans. According to psychiatrist Carl Jung, "Hurry is not *of* the Devil; it *is* the Devil."

Admittedly, as my children have gotten older, it has become more difficult to resist these productive, "super" temptations. My boys are interested in more activities, and we have had to think carefully about what we are willing to commit to. However, we still control our schedule and leave plenty of time to kick off our shoes and breathe deeply. Once again I think of the well-credentialed Betsy: "By doing nothing and by finally trying to quiet ourselves, we can start to move inside and really connect with our true essence, our higher self, or perhaps something even larger."

Perhaps it is during these moments—these periods of calm— that we'll hear God's voice and his powerful stirring inside us. Maybe it is during these restful breaths that we'll become more open to those around us and find more compassion for their needs. When we bring this sense of calm, this deep and holy presence, to our moms' group, our purpose will appear sharper. We'll be a group of mamas—fiery because of our calm—wide open to the world, to God's promptings, and ready for action.

One group that has historically stressed the need to enter into listening silences is the Quakers. The Quakers are also known for their social action. I know several creative Quaker mothers who seem to have a knack for balance. They keep peace in their homes while simultaneously striving to do the same out in the world. William Penn wrote in *No Cross, No Crown* that "true godliness does not turn men out of the world, but enables them to live better in it and excites their endeavors to mend it."[5] Which is precisely why this seemingly odd chapter in praise of doing *nothing* in a book encouraging mothers to get up and do *something* actually makes a small bit of sense. In fact, I believe the correlation is direct and profound. In Exodus 14:14, it is written that the Lord will fight for us; we need only to be still. We can practice being in the presence of the Lord by slowing down our lives and striving for simplicity. By simplifying the ins and outs of our everyday lives, we have more time to ponder big ideas and more energy to spend on the things that drive the kingdom of God.

The more I have come to understand the connection between acting in love and in laziness, the more I am convinced that I want to lead a simpler, "lazier" life. To me, this life is slow and intentional. It's a style of existence that makes room for God's voice and has time for holy promptings. It's a life not controlled by things or a strict schedule, but rather by relationships and more time to be prayerful and thoughtful. A simple life allows us more time to notice our neighbors—to love them and serve them and learn from them. It allows for more moments of listening to the stir of our hearts. It allows more time to dream of ways to make a difference in the world and more space to start planning and executing. Before there are grand gestures, there needs to be room to breathe. And to think, this can all begin from your perch on the couch, coffee cup in hand, children linking Legos in the corner.

I have to admit that all of this is easier said than done. I have talked to my friends, my husband, psychologists, scientists, and spiritual advisors alike in an attempt to reinforce this idea because, in essence, it is countercultural. We are led to believe that we must be *more* in order to be happy. We need to *do more* and we need to *be more* and we need to *consume more* . . . these are the messages that culture drowns us with daily. We live in a culture of more.

Our children are not immune. Pick up a typical parenting magazine, and you'll soon be convinced (if you're not already) that your children need more as well. They need more educational toys, Newbery-honored books, early education and exploratory classes. Chinese for Tots, Suzuki violin, and YMCA Toddler Tumbling all on Tuesday? No problem. We'd rather run ourselves ragged than risk our precious child falling behind. Panic strikes when we hear that the child next door is taking (and I am only slightly joking) French Pastry for Preschoolers. We are quick to jump to the conclusion that our children, just like ourselves, need to *be more* and *have more* in order to succeed in this world.

When it all gets to be too much and we find ourselves needing a little pick-me-up, we go shopping to accumulate more shoes or a new blouse or a pair of throw pillows to repair our damaged spirits. We dream of life with leather seats and longer, more lavish vacations. All of this, you would think by scrolling through Instagram or flipping through a magazine, would lead to utter contentment and happiness. But is this really so?

My husband and I left the city of Chicago seeking closer relationships to our family who lived in the community to which we hoped to move. I'll be honest, we also sought more space for our children to roam. We wanted more than what we could conceive our city life to offer. In many ways, this has worked out well for our family. However, there are drawbacks.

When we moved out of our small, one-and-a-half bedroom city apartment where four of us were living, we didn't have a lot of stuff. It simply didn't fit. We had to be careful what we purchased, because we didn't have space to store much. The house we moved into has two floors, four bedrooms, a backyard, and a garage. As you can imagine, like any good, middle-class, God-fearing American family, we have managed to fill it with things. Such things, of course, require money and attention and care. Essentially, moving from a barely two-bedroom apartment to a four-bedroom house means that we have a lot more cleaning to do. We also spend more time pushing a mower. Time that we now spend vacuuming and dusting our two floors of living space used to be spent exploring the city or sitting on our stoop chatting with neighbors. I suppose you could say we have achieved a common perception of the American dream, but it has come at a cost.

I experience the same sort of awakening of the ugly cost of *more* during the week between Christmas and New Year's Eve, which includes not only the holidays, but our son's birthday and the anniversary of our wedding. It's a big week for our family—one that I always hope to treat like a great big party with pans of hot lasagna and kettles of steaming oyster stew and doting aunts and boisterous uncles and a ridiculous amount of laughter. We typically accomplish this, but it always comes with a bit of a sting.

I find that I spend a lot of time the week between Christmas and New Year's—time that I would prefer to devote solely to relationships and celebrating—managing stuff. In order to make room for the new toys, we must sort through the old. Toys are bursting out of toy boxes, clothes are bursting out of drawers, books are hanging off of bookshelves. I appreciate the generosity and the genuine love of giving and seeing each other happy and excited, but managing the pile of stuff that results sucks both time and energy that I would rather spend in community eating pie with the people I love.

Perhaps it's just me, but I tend to notice that the less clutter surrounds me, the less cluttered my mind is. When my mind is not consumed with of-the-moment, worldly details, I am more able to focus on what God has given. When not wading through piles and managing mess, I can see my gifts and the ways I can use them to work for good. When I am not managing things or doing mountains of laundry (how many pairs of pants does one child really need?) after I put my children to bed for the evening, I can read books or work on my current life-giving project. I can sit down and concentrate on a conversation with my husband or write a note to a friend. The less clutter I have around me, the more I find my priorities align with the gospel.

William Channing, an American writer and theologian who lived and wrote in the early 1800s, said this:

To live content with small means.
To seek elegance rather than luxury,

and refinement rather than fashion.
To be worthy not respectable,
    and wealthy not rich.
To study hard, think quietly, talk gently,
    act frankly, to listen to stars, birds, babes,
    and sages with open heart, to bear all cheerfully,
    do all bravely, await occasions, hurry never.
In a word, to let the spiritual,
    unbidden and unconscious,
    grow up through the common.
This is my symphony.[6]

Considering that these words were written by Channing two hundred years ago—and yet have overcome the expanse of time—I believe that we are not the only generation to struggle. These words inspire me. But what does it mean to live this way as a child of God in a culture of excess and consumerism and shininess and the quest for more?

By no means am I the wealthiest person in my neighborhood, but I do enjoy incredible privilege, and that is very important to acknowledge. First of all, I have a minivan that I can drive all over town if I want to. This is simple, but such a luxury. For me, a trip to Target or the grocery store or wherever does not require a long walk or a couple of transfers on the city bus. Convenience is mine.

I have access to superior health care. If my children are sick, they go to the doctor. I get annual exams, and when I picked up a parasite after a trip to Ethiopia, I was tested and treated at minimum expense. When my husband had a toothache, he simply went to the dentist to have it repaired. I have clean water flowing from my two bathroom and kitchen faucets. (And I have two bathrooms [!] in my air-conditioned, heated home.) As you know, this is not the case in most of the world, or even in all of the United States.

Like you, I am literate. I was offered a public education in which I was given books to read and technology to explore. Now I go to the library and the bookstore to acquire books about things in which I'm interested. When I have a question and need a quick answer, I can open my laptop and hop on the Internet. I have clothes for myself and for my children. When our cupboards are approaching bare, I simply make a trip to the grocery store or the market and purchase fruits and vegetables, and I even spring for organic products if I feel so moved. Such a lifestyle is a thing of dreams in other places throughout my own city, let alone the world.

It gets even more unbelievable: I actually pay someone else to pour my coffee several times a week, just like I pay someone to cut and highlight my hair every couple of months. I occasionally get a pedicure. My family goes out for dinner regularly and we enjoy cooking elaborate meals—sometimes with specialty ingredients—at home. On the Global Rich List (www.globalrichlist.com), my family ranks in the top one percent of the richest people in the world. I would be willing to bet that yours does, too.

I am beyond grateful for all of these gifts. Yet I am cognizant of the fact that not everyone can live the way we do. I praise God and the universe for winning the lottery of life; I try to always be thankful. I try to do as Paul enthusiastically instructs in his letter to the Philippians, especially 3:17–4:9. "Celebrate God all day, every day," he writes. "I mean *revel* in him!" (Phil. 4:4 *The Message*). But in addition to such praise, I'd like to take this love and these unbelievable blessings, and use them to make someone else's day a little bit easier.

When I consider these truths and see these things spelled out in front of me, I realize how silly it is, then, to think I need more means or more luxury in my life. It seems ridiculous to think I need new boots or a kitchen upgrade or another pair of yoga pants, as I often become convinced. And yet the temptation is constantly there, and I need constant reminding that less is in fact more. I need reinforcement because I constantly fail. Seek contentment. Live with small means. Hurry never. I need Channing's words to be tattooed on my hand.

His words are not tattooed on my hand, or anywhere else on my body for that matter, but I do have a similar reminder framed and hanging in my kitchen, which, like many mothers throughout space and time, is the room that I spend much of my time in at home. Yes, as the cherry on top of the privilege cake, I recently purchased a letter-pressed print created by Sussex artists Lesley and Pea. I am drawn to the plucky "Aardvaark Manifesto 2010" and reference it often as I pass time in the kitchen:

> **KILL YOUR TV.**
> BAKE CAKE. DRINK TEA.
> **PLAY A KAZOO.**
> CHOOSE HANDMADE. LOVE YOUR TOWN.
> **SING. KEEP IT WONKY.**
> BARTER AND SWAP.
> **MAKE STUFF. WRITE LETTERS.**
> **CHAMPION** THE UNDERDOG.
> GROW YOUR **COMMUNITY**.
> **LOVE** ALL THE **PEOPLE.**
> LIVE YOUR LIFE.
> **BE KIND.**

To me, this print answers James's question when he probes us to consider what our lives are truly about. "You do not even know what will happen tomorrow," he says. "What is your life? You are a mist that appears for a little while and then vanishes" (4:14).

The life I want to lead is of my true self. It's not super-sized and it's not swimming in stuff. Instead, it's one rich with friendship. As my friend Clark says, a life worth living is a life of eternal significance. It's a life of kindness and generosity. A life of love. Because we truly don't know what is going to happen tomorrow; we often hear it said that we might best live today as if we're dying. What would you do if this were actually true?

Personally, I'd like to think that I would keep things simple. I'd like to think that I would bake a cake for my family, drink coffee with friends, do something silly like play a kazoo, and live my day for God and for good.

I would like to think that I could focus on, as Jesus taught (and Lesley and Pea suggest in attractive block lettering), being kind and loving all the people. Perhaps I'd find some adrenaline with my moms' group as I worked with my friends on a project meant to shower love into our corner of the world. I would like to think that I would be willing to fight for this—that I would keep working to fight off Supermom and all of her promptings. That I'd squash my worldly impulses and that I wouldn't spend all my time cleaning for appearance's sake or shopping for new things. I want to love all people. I don't want perfection or clutter, or the quest to look good on my social media feeds, to get in the way of that.

The sad truth is that people *are* dying today. And too often their deaths are both senseless and preventable. Today alone, 4,500 children will die due to their lack of access to clean water. Nearly three thousand children will perish from malaria. This doesn't have to be. By living simply, I can take my wealth, my education, my good health and energy—all of my abundance—and make it work in the world. I can take the money that I save by not purchasing a new set of throw pillows and send it to a poverty-fighting organization that I believe in. I can look for gifts that are fair trade or that support an organizational goal. I can use my education to learn about pressing issues and uncover worthy solutions. After paring down and prioritizing my schedule, I can use the time I have saved to volunteer in meaningful ways. I can live simply, as Mother Teresa says, so that others may simply live.

A pared-down existence will not only change the ways we live our days as individuals, but it will also directly impact the way we live as part of a community. We will make room in our schedules for good, faithful work. We will make room in our minds for spiritual promptings. We might literally make room in our homes and bank accounts, turning our excess into solutions for the hurting people of this world.

In his book *The Purpose Driven Life*, Rick Warren writes that "you can give without loving, but you cannot love without giving. Love means giving up—yielding my preferences, comfort, goals, security, money, energy, or time for the benefit of someone else."[7] Such an expectation might make us nervous. We might fret, as I do, that our children will someday be disappointed by our choice to limit their schedule or shop in thrift stores. We may be plagued by the feeling that we are squandering personal comfort by giving away clothing or household items or by simply not taking the time to shop for them in the first place. We will find that it takes strength to live lives that at times seem countercultural.

The apostle Paul realized the need to leave behind his credentials, comforts, and the trappings of his past in order to follow the teachings of Jesus. He knew that there was change to be had and an element of sacrifice involved. He looked ahead to the future and did not dwell on what he was missing or leaving behind; rather, he compared his work and life to a race and chose to focus on the finish line and on knowing and loving Jesus. He encourages us to do the same in his letter to the Philippians. "Forgetting what is behind and straining toward what is ahead," he writes, "I press on toward the goal to win the prize for which God has called me heavenward in Christ Jesus" (3:13–14).

It didn't matter that Paul had to give up his reputation as a highly educated, respected Jewish rabbi and Roman citizen in order to trumpet the joys of Jesus. His goal was to serve and give like Jesus. He let go of who he used to be and what society expected of him in order to move forward with a focus on loving like Jesus. When it comes down to it, we too have to give up some worldly security and swagger in order to love and serve like Jesus. Surrounding yourself with women who are striving for the same goal will help make this sacrifice seem like no sacrifice at all.

A simpler life will mean something different for everyone. Not all of us are going to feel called to give up our large homes and closets. Not all of us have the luxury of finding more time in our schedules. Not all of us can quit lifestyle habits on a dime. However, we can all become more mindful of what we consume and where we spend our energy and perhaps make changes gradually. Perhaps it may quite literally begin with a moms' group rummage sale to raise money to give away to those in need. In the process of decluttering, homes will be simplified. Both literally and figuratively, loads will be lightened. Different moms' groups will find different ways to embrace the philosophy of living simply, both financially and emotionally. Together, you'll have to discern what it will mean for you and your community. The road might be patchy, but it will be worth courageously exploring.

For my family, striving for simplicity plays out in many different ways. My husband and I do not spend more money than we make and we budget what we earn very closely. Our home, though very nice, is a hundred years old and shows its wear. We live on a beautiful, tree-lined street filled with working-class people. The school that we send our children to is an absolute gem, though on paper it is "poor" and low-achieving.

Though we have acquired what seems to me to be a ridiculous amount of things, we try to either buy things used or share things like tools and lawn-care equipment with our friends and family. I love fashion, but I shop thrift stores first or buy well-made clothes that I know I'll wear for years. In fact, my children have been complimented many times over for their unique, edgy style, and I secretly love the fact that it literally cost quarters at the local Salvation Army resale store.

We have a kitchen garden during the summer months, and though we enjoy eating well and will certainly splurge on restaurant meals, we do most of our dining at home. Jake and I make a lot of the things we eat from scratch because it is less expensive than buying it at the store. (Why buy organic peanut butter when you can easily make it at home for a fraction of the cost?) I have been able to do a lot of these things because I have been at home with my children, and for years the work that I have done could happen during naptime, in the early morning hours, or in the evenings. Though I could certainly work more and earn a larger income, the things I busy myself with at home are money-saving and, I believe, valuable.

Don't get me wrong—we do not deprive ourselves of good times, small indulgences, and even great vacations, but we are intentionally moderate in our consumption. We certainly do not do this perfectly and we often find ourselves off course and in need of reprioritization, but we do try to use our talents, position, and gifts in ways that open up more time and resources to give freely as we strive to love others better.

Supermom will try to get in your way as you simplify your life. She might talk you out of giving away part of last winter's wardrobe by allowing the thought of being without an extra fallback sweater to seem frightening. She might convince you to hop on Amazon and spend a lot of money on things that you don't need, simply for an emotional lift. Supermom might try to take over your schedule, hijacking the ability to squeeze another hour out of the day in which to help someone in need or stealing the time planned for personal enrichment and growth through study or meditation or meaningful conversation with a friend. Supermom might try, but she won't win. A simple, more meaningful life will get in her way. A richer life filled with joyful sacrifice, with community, and with love. Support one another in this endeavor, because when all is said and done, living simply can be pretty super after all.

NOTES

[1]Much has been written about the importance of play in the development of children. Here are a few articles that discuss the benefits of unstructured free time: Katrina Schwartz, "How Free Play Can Define Kids' Success," *Mind/Shift*, February 15, 2013, accessed July 25, 2016, http://ww2.kqed.org/mindshift/2013 /02/15/how-free-play-can-define-kids-success/. John Hamilton, "Scientists Say Child's Play Helps Built a Better Brain," *NPR*, August 4, 2014, accessed July 25, 2016, http://www.npr.org/sections/ed/2014/08/06/336361277/scientists-say -childs-play-helps-build-a-better-brain. K. J. Dell'Antonia, "Protect Your Child's 'PDF:' Playtime, Downtime, and Family Time," *New York Times*, January 4, 2016, accessed July 25, 2016, http://parenting.blogs.nytimes.com /2016/01/04/the-lessons-of-winter-break-protect-playtime-downtime-and -family-time/.

[2]If you're interested in making meditation part of your worship practice, I love the app Headspace. www.headspace.com.

[3]Richard Foster, *Celebration of Discipline* (San Francisco: HarperCollins, 1998), 20.

[4]Ibid., 27.

[5]William Penn, *No Cross, No Crown: A Discourse* (Philadelphia: T. K. & P. G. Collins, 1853), 61.

[6]William Henry Channing, *My Symphony.* Public domain.

[7]Rick Warren, *The Purpose Driven Life* (Grand Rapids: Zondervan, 2011), 128.

CHAPTER NINE

Do Good

> Dismiss the voices of perfection and competition.
> They are loud but quite unenlightened.
> They'd have you waste your entire life.
> —Glennon Melton Doyle

In order for each of our Mama Bears to use her righteous anger in bold and beautiful ways and stride toward vibrant and productive social change, much work must be done on the inside. Until then, her gait is slow and clumsy. For me, unleashing my Mama Bear in healthy and productive ways requires putting Supermom in the corner and unlocking the chains of perfection. After years of conversations discussing the shackles of perfectionism, I've come to believe that I am not alone in this struggle and that it's something humans have struggled with throughout time. As Voltaire, the French writer, thinker, and philosopher cautions, "Don't let the perfect be the enemy of the good."

Deep in our family lore are stories of how I first learned to walk. My mother will gently remind me of the process every once in a while when, say, we're standing in her kitchen preparing a meal and she senses impatience, or when I relate over the phone that the grip of perfection is once again tightening.

The story goes something like this: a cautious, determined child with strawberry-blonde curls and ample cheeks, I spent a few weeks during my eleventh month sliding along the furniture in our apartment, just as many children do as they secure their footing in the world. Once I felt steady on my feet and wanted to explore further, I allowed someone to hold my hand while I toddled along. I was walking, my mom recalls. I could walk! The world was my oyster and I was on my way to great things! But if my trusted guide tried to shake my chubby hand away and encourage me to take a step on my own, I promptly sat down on the ground and refused to go further.

In time, I grew more confident and would allow my guide to provide security by extending one finger rather than the whole hand. With this crutch, I cruised with confidence. I would smile in delight at my newfound ability. "Look at Leslie," my mother would exclaim joyfully. "She's walking!" But if the finger was taken away, I planted my little bottom firmly on the ground and refused to move.

Eventually it was a mere touch of the hand. If my finger touched your palm, I was good to go and could stroll all day. Remove the skin-to-skin contact and I was sitting on my bum, frustrated with my fickle chaperone.

And then, as my mother tells it, one day I walked across the living room, as if I'd been walking my entire life.

I didn't take a few steps, fall down, and then get up to try it again. One day I crawled and the next day I walked. Until I was absolutely, 100 percent confident that I could do it right . . . *perfectly* and *by myself* . . . I refused to try. My perfectionism was already terrorizing me. I've been fighting it ever since.

I recall this story here because in serving those around us, we don't need to wait until the moment we are able to show up and perform perfectly. This may take months—years even, depending on our expectations of ourselves—or it may never happen, and that's precious time wasted. We don't have to wait until the moment we've got it all together and can handle it 100 percent efficiently and effectively. Our loving actions don't need to take the shape of a medal-winning sprint; in fact, a slow and steady gait will do just fine. So just in case you can relate to any of these stubborn or precision-prone tendencies that are sometimes revealed even in infancy, it bears repeating here: you have a strong community; a fervent prayer; a well-established purpose; an incredible, life-giving talent; and a detailed plan. It's time to make it happen. Get up and walk, baby. You can do this. You can do *something*.

Dropping off a bottle of wine to Cynthia, just to let her know that I'm thinking of her in her time of transition or dissonance, might mean a great deal to her. I may not, in one particular moment or season, have time to prepare a made-from-scratch dinner for a family with a newborn, but I can certainly swing by the store for a take-and-bake pizza, a box of baby lettuce, and a container of fresh fruit. Such gestures, which cost me little in terms of time and money, may affect the recipient in profound ways. Proverbs 3:27–28 (GNT) tells us, "Whenever you possibly can, do good to those who need it. Never tell your neighbors to wait until tomorrow if you can help them now."

God gives his love freely and we need to follow his lead. God creates us in a holy image, puts people in our lives to be loved and to love us, and provides for our every need. As we have the opportunity, we should do good to all people (Gal. 6:10). We don't need to do *perfect* to all people, we just need to be creative and loving and we need to do *good*.

Too many great ideas and beautiful intentions are fast to fall by the wayside. I have to be honest. I sometimes come up with decent ideas but then struggle greatly with follow-through. For instance, while at the grocery store I run into my friend Joel. He tells me that his dog has just died. I make a note to myself to be available for a phone call or to send a note of sympathy and encouragement his way. I leave with the best intentions but then forget all about them as I get swept up into my day and my other obligations. It doesn't have to be so.

Just because your moms' group might not have the means, organization, or energy to pull off a large-scale banquet or the charity event of the year, it doesn't mean you aren't impacting our world in big and meaningful ways. If you manage to feed or clothe a few, you've done good work. You don't have to be wealthy. You don't have to have perfect circumstances to make a difference. So often in the early years of motherhood, I find myself thinking, "I'll do that once the kids are in school." Or, "Maybe when we make just a bit more money, I'll start giving more." There is a litany of reasons not to do something right now, but this sort of thinking is impaired. With a little creativity, I can love better and have more fun right at this very moment. My circumstances might not seem ideal for big waves of change, but they are, in this moment, perfect for God's case in the world.

Both Mark (12:41–44) and Luke (21:1–4) recount a story in which Jesus takes notice of a woman with a beautiful heart. This woman makes no excuses for who she is or for her place in life. She captures Jesus's attention by doing everything and nothing all at once. Mark paints the scene like this:

> Jesus sat down opposite the place where the offerings
> were put and watched the crowd putting their money
> into the temple treasury. Many rich people threw in

large amounts. But a poor widow came and put in two very small copper coins, worth only a few cents. Calling his disciples to him, Jesus said, "Truly I tell you, this poor widow has put more into the treasury than all the others. They all gave out of their wealth; but she, out of her poverty, put in everything—all she had to live on."

Your everything might not seem like a very big deal to those watching. In fact, your everything might not seem like much at all, especially compared to the seemingly "bigger" work of others. Giving out of your own version of poverty might not be flashy or even that outwardly impactful. The Bill and Melinda Gates Foundation may never notice you, neither Oprah nor Ellen may ever congratulate you, and you may never garner community-wide attention. With children at home, you might not have as much time as you'd ideally like to finish a project. You might not have as much money as you would like to fund materials. You simply may not have the energy you need to give it your typical gold-star standard. But none of these things should stop you from doing the best you can. Offer your "everything" with all the love you can muster. Then fall into bed exhausted by loving the world as best you could.

Gretchen Rubin, author of *The Happiness Project*, relates to this idea in terms of story. She wisely tells readers that she "didn't want to be like the novelist who spent so much time rewriting his first sentence that he never wrote the second."[1] Remember this as you and your moms dare to do good. Your life is your novel, and this is the story of extravagant generosity and an attempt to live and love like Jesus. Don't get caught up in the first line.

If Rubin had not moved on, she wouldn't have written a really great book. If my friend Cathy hadn't gotten over her fear that no one would come to the ice-cream-social fundraiser that she hosts each summer on her flower farm, she wouldn't have been able to support the organizations that rely on small contributions from big-hearted community members over the years. If the group of mothers who volunteer at a local elementary school in my community had spent all of their energy worrying about whether or not they served the "right" food or filled the event space with Pinterest-perfect decorations at their trivia-night fundraiser, they never would have been able to merrily raise enough money to send a dozen city kids to summer camp who wouldn't have had the chance otherwise.

By taking the plunge, we can creatively offer everything and make a huge dent. We can do the best that we can with the tools and abilities we have. We can identify our poverty (Is it time? Is it money?) and we can give from what we do have. Who knows what you might be able to do? I wouldn't put anything past a group of riled-up Mama Bears. And maybe the ripple effects of your ministry will touch thousands. This wouldn't surprise me, either. Think about the women in your moms' group. I'd guess that they're pretty amazing. I wouldn't bet against you.

And yet you don't have to reach thousands. Your impact may be just as profound if you pool your resources and cover a single mother's rent for a month. Getting together to arrange vases of flowers for a local nursing home could bring more joy than you might think. Imagine the stories those recipients will tell. Think of how they will be touched by your small offering of love. Simple acts can have profound effects.

"Don't let the perfect be the enemy of the good," I tell myself again. And even though it strikes terror in my Virgo heart, it's prudent advice. Not everything your moms' group comes up with is going to come together exactly as it was envisioned in the initial brainstorming session. Sometimes it will. Sometimes the pieces will fall into place and the right people will show up and the outcome will be absolutely astounding. But other times the ripples will be smaller and less shiny.

It might be tempting to disregard the project if it is not up to your high standards. Make a pact with your girlfriends not to let this happen. What is simply good to you may seem just exactly right to someone else. Done with love, your effort will demonstrate God's heart. Don't shortchange someone a kindness simply because it doesn't shine like gold in your eyes. Don't shortchange yourself the act of loving the world. Walk on—humbly and with God. And refuse to allow what you perceive to be perfect become the enemy of what you know to be profoundly and breathtakingly good.

NOTE

[1]Gretchen Rubin, *The Happiness Project* (New York: HarperCollins, 2009), 78.

PART FOUR

A bear won't wonder,
"Gee, do I attack, do I run?"
It just acts. . . .
You can't outrun them,
you can't outwit them,
you can't out-anything them.

—*Backpacker Magazine*

CHAPTER TEN

Deeply Flawed and Deeply Faithful

> The ultimate measure of a [wo]man is not where [s]he
> stands in moments of comfort and convenience, but where
> [s]he stands at times of challenge and controversy.
> —Dr. Martin Luther King Jr.

As many joyful moments as you are sure to share with your tribe of women, there will be seasons when relationships will require some extra work and when goodwill projects will stall. By anticipating these moments, you will be better prepared to handle each challenge with maturity and grace. The following is a list of nine common hurdles that your moms' group may face and possible solutions for keeping on track in relationships, integrity, and the work that you do in your community and the world.

Challenge #1—The group loses sight of its purpose.

The purpose of your moms' group must be closely guarded. You'll find that it will always be easier *not* to get up and work on loving those around you in deep and meaningful ways. When things seem daunting and challenging and out of our comfort zone, we all know that it would be much simpler if we could just skip them altogether. It's also easier to keep relationships on the surface rather than do the work necessary to really get to know one another. However, by limiting our vision or losing sight of what is possible, we miss out on a tremendous amount of goodness.

There are so many reasons it is easier to simply meet together as a moms' group to discuss the ins and outs of everyday life without ever exploring the possibility of being the hands and feet of Christ in the larger world. It's so much easier to dream about ways to rattle the world than it is to get around to being the change you wish to see. And just as there is an array of topics to distract from the matter at hand—which is to make the world a better place by harnessing Mama Bear and using the sphere of your collective influence for good—there are a thousand reasons that great ideas and good intentions might be able to wait.

Don't buy the excuses. Do not bow down to the pressure of a greater culture. No one ever said that a life devoted to Jesus would be easy. Soul enriching? Yes. A walk in the park? No. Doing good work may be inconvenient. It may be uncomfortable. It may be difficult and stressful and downright hard. As Brennan Manning writes in *Abba's Child*, "The unwounded life bears no resemblance to the Rabbi."[1]

Thankfully, if you're struggling as an individual through a particularly rough patch and don't have the energy to keep focused on what your group aspires to be, your sisters will be there to lift you up. We come to our moms' group and our life of Christ together. As part of one body, it is simply not necessary for one person to carry all of the weight. If one of us begins to meander, another will lead her back with encouragement and love. If one of us feels like throwing in the towel, another will catch it, launder it, and hand it back fresh, folded, and infused with new enthusiasm.

Realize your meaningful purpose by making sure the group has a backbone. You each need to be accountable to one another to put a halt to conversations shrouded in negativity. Gently dismiss the reasons that are getting in the way of your kingdom work and look often to your purpose as a missional moms' community. Support one another; lift each other up. Encourage and inspire . . . and live your priorities. Together, you've established your vision and your purpose and you genuinely aspire to good in the world— now live up to your big ideas and hold fast to your bottom line. As is written in Proverbs, don't put off until tomorrow what you can do today (3:27–28).

Challenge #2—You fail to recognize the seasons.
However.

It should go without saying: if you have a new baby, you need not participate in your moms' group's latest fundraising effort. If you are nine months pregnant, please don't volunteer to stay on your feet all day baking. If you have a clingy two-year-old who requires your undivided attention all day long, let someone else screen print the T-shirts. If you have several energetic toddlers or even an emotionally draining teenager, don't tell your moms' group that you will be the one to shop for supplies or shoulder the public relations.

Rather, be realistic about what you can accomplish both as an individual and as a group. The great thing about a moms' group is that you are a community of people who can lean on one another, support one another, shore up each other's faith, and work together for good. Just as one of you is busy cuddling a newborn, another among you is basking in the energy of her second trimester. Just as one has a pair of preschoolers, another is embracing a new-found freedom as she sends all of her children off to school each morning. Be honest with yourselves and with each other about what you can and cannot take on, thus being careful not to over-burden one another.

I often have conversations with my mom friends about our ever-evolving priorities. We discuss how before we had babies we used to go for walks or meet at the movies when we found ourselves with a free moment. This rarely happens anymore; we are simply living in a different season of life. This plays out in many facets. For instance, when my boys were four and six years old, I was able to visit multiple grocery stores every couple of weeks in order to shop for the best products and deals for our family without much drama. I would go to the health-food store for bulk goods, Miss Effie's Flower Farm for fresh eggs, Sam's Club (my town's equivalent of Costco) for chocolate chips and cheese, and the standard grocery for everything else. When we added a very energetic little sister to the mix, I stuck to one store for all of our needs, under-standing that though I may have been accustomed to purchasing specialty goods and saving a bit of money by being a pickier shop-per, it was no longer worth the hassle. Similarly, another friend has expressed interest in learning how to can fruits and vegetables at the end of the growing season; however, with five kids under the age of eight, she is realistic about what she can and cannot get done during this particular stretch of life.

On the other side of the spectrum, there is a group of women at my church who get together and call themselves the Empty Nesters. They, too, have found themselves in a new season and are gather-ing together to offer each other support and companionship. Their children are grown and living on their own, and these women have entered a whole new stage of parenting their adult children. I'm anxious to see what they do with their new position. Will they mentor new moms? Use their lack of carpool duties to start shut-tling Meals on Wheels? With each new phase of life come new excitement and new opportunities to serve; we just need to be mindful about the timing.

Challenge #3—Backlash beats you down.

A few years ago, I read a newspaper article about frazzled mothers who had gotten caught up in too much volunteer work.[2] It featured a woman who declared that she was constantly stressed and completely overscheduled because of the volunteer work she committed to at her children's school. After realizing that she no longer had time to help her children with their school projects because she was too busy with her own school projects, she (with strong encouragement from her husband) started guarding her time and saying no to requests for more.

This is particularly relevant today, as many American women have greater flexibility in the work that we do outside of the home. Many of us work for ourselves, or the work that we do is flexible and quite possibly done from our own address. Furthermore, we are educated, competent workers who have reputations for getting things done well. Because of this flexibility and ability, people often ask for our time, and it can be hard to set basic boundaries. Many of us are people pleasers and find it difficult to say no, even if what is being requested of us is not really in the best interest of our families or ourselves.

Suppose you have taken time off from work to care for your children full-time, or you've arranged your part-time work schedule so that you can be there for your family, but then you say yes to every phone call petitioning your help and reply affirmatively to emails asking to add your name to lists for baked goods for the bazaar or a spot on the hallway decorations team at your child's school. We can celebrate the PTO president who spends dozens of hours a week planning events and rallying the troops to support the school. Some of us are made for this role. Others only do it because they feel obligated or simply cannot muster the perspective or courage to say no. If you're not careful about your priorities, you can lose sight of the life you had envisioned. You can easily run yourself ragged under the guise of doing good.

And it's not just your children's school that will draw you in. If you start looking, you'll find countless ways to use your gifts and talents for good. Nearly any nonprofit you come across would love for you to show up a couple of times a week to stuff envelopes or provide support. Underresourced schools will seek you out to eat lunch and discuss books with students. Your church probably offers countless ways for you to serve. There are political and community events to organize and attend. There is no shortage of ways for the civic minded with a little time on their hands to engage in the community.

All of these great opportunities are valid and would surely benefit from your presence. Many may turn out to be great experiences for you as well. However, even in the world of philanthropy, charity, and volunteerism, it's dangerous to try to do it all.

Narrowing down the areas in which you are willing to serve will allow you to make a bigger impact and enjoy the experience more. Just as I recommend writing a statement of mission and vision for your moms' group, I have also found that writing a personal mission statement is helpful in making decisions about where and when to help. If I get a particularly convincing plea for my time and talent, I often refer back to my mission statement. I am particularly passionate about literacy and clean water. Knowing this helps me determine where I am willing to spend my energy.

I also know where my gifts lie. Trust me when I say that you don't want me to fumble over words on the phone asking for money or volunteers or support. I am inarticulate and uncomfortable on the phone. However, I can write a great press release or come up with creative marketing material in a snap. My personal mission statement also keeps me from getting caught off guard. It helps me say no to some things so that I can say yes to the opportunities that I am better suited for and more interested in. Knowing your passions and gifts will help you identify the tasks that will bring you pleasure and at which you will be most effective. It will also help you to prioritize.

By narrowing your scope and fine-tuning your interests and skills, you can contribute in ways which are more valuable and more fulfilling. This, too, will allow you the time and energy needed for your family—not to mention the moms' group you are committed to.

Challenge #4—Loving your sister is not always easy.

Relationships require hard work. It's as simple and as complex as that. Your mama friendships are no exception. In fact, when you engage with one another at an intentionally intense level, it is especially important to protect your friendships and keep them functioning healthfully.

Among even our closest friendships we can expect that there will be occasional squabbles, disagreements, and hurt feelings. Your moms' group might as well plan on it and therefore commit early on to working on the dynamics of these important relationships. I find great confidence and joy in the fact that my mom friends will love me despite my shortcomings. I am thankful that even though I am horrible at picking up the phone and calling as often as I should, they love me regardless. They've loved me on days when they've witnessed me being a less-than-stellar parent and on days when I've said hurtful things or retreated rather than saying what needed to be said. They have offered me grace, love, and forgiveness over and over again. This is no small thing; it has required patience and understanding. Unless the relationship is abusive or unhealthy in a way that cannot be remedied, we should work to live richly in community with our mom friends.

When you love like sisters, life together will be rich, though sometimes difficult. You will disagree with one another and sometimes feel resentful. Jealousy or envy may seep in. It is only natural that when engaging in authentic relationship, there may be moments of conflict. When children are involved, the possibilities can intensify because of all the added dynamics and relationships thrown into the mix. At one of our annual "Chicago moms' group" summer gatherings (brazenly and adorably named Mommapalooza and complete with bright T-shirts and a bounce house for the kids), I watched as some of my favorite people's shoulders slumped while listening to stories of success about the children among us.

"Your child already knows how to read? Mine is not even close!" someone would say with a twinge of what I could sense was mama guilt.

Because we have committed to keeping our relationships healthy, we do our best to be sensitive to one another. And because we know each other well enough to be honest with one another, all it took to get us back on track was for someone to say, "Hey, let's not compare. We're all doing what we think is best for our kids." Comparison is something we have to protect our relationships from. Friendships can survive as long as we're willing to rise above our own pettiness and insecurity and are willing to forgive one another as well as celebrate one another.

Sister Joan Chittister writes that "the living of the gospel life is not an individual enterprise of private whim and flights of personal fancy but a conscious gathering of the wisdom of others who can encourage us and help us scrutinize our own choices for their value and their valor."[3] Your moms' group can provide a home to such wisdom . . . a safe place where you can help one another grow as mothers, people, and Christ-followers. You'll know that you have reached a wonderful place in your relationships when you begin to genuinely worry for each other and look out for one another's well-being. You'll have conquered jealousy and immaturity, and you'll experience the joy of true friendship. By reading Scripture, praying with one another, having honest conversation, and being open to living out the gospel, you will grow in wisdom and love with one another. This is worth protecting with all of your might.

> Be devoted to one another in love. Honor one another above yourselves. Never be lacking in zeal, but keep your spiritual fervor, serving the Lord. Be joyful in hope, patient in affliction, faithful in prayer. Share with the Lord's people who are in need. Practice hospitality. Bless those who persecute you; bless and do not curse. Rejoice with those who rejoice; mourn with those who mourn. Live in harmony with one another. (Rom. 12:10–16)

Challenge #5—We begin to believe that love and success are finite.

Let's reiterate.

In a world set up to make quick comparisons that ultimately pit people against each other, it's easy to fall into the habit of envy rather than celebration, of treating each other harshly rather than with appreciation and civility. The notion that one woman's climb to the top will hinder our own, or that another woman's great idea makes our idea insignificant, is flawed—yet commonplace. It seems that social media, for all of its benefits, can sometimes lure the ugly beast of comparison. A photo of a friend's recent success posted on Facebook, for example, too often breeds jealousy rather than congratulations. It doesn't have to be this way.

Liberian Nobel Peace Prize winner Leymah Gbowee tells a powerful story of women working together and creating an unstoppable force of goodness in her book, *Mighty Be Our Powers: How Sisterhood, Prayer, and Sex Changed a Nation at War.* In 2003, Gbowee organized and led Women of Liberia Mass Action for Peace, a coalition of women who harnessed their anger and hardship to work for peace. Gbowee surrounded herself with strong, compassionate women, and they were all empowered through support and collaboration. They ultimately helped stop a corrupt president, menacing warlords, and a civil war. "If any changes were to be made in society it had to be by the mothers," she wrote in her book, recognizing the power of a fully realized group of Mama Bears who were *for* each other.

Harriett Tubman fled slavery and then went back to the south to usher hundreds of other women to freedom, showing not only courage, but also a deep care of others. Tina Fey and Amy Poehler write comedy with a specific message, which Poehler explained by saying, "You can create your own spark. And if you have another woman to support you, you can be very, very powerful."[4]

We can learn a lot from each other, particularly from those who are champions of meaningful pursuits and unbridled potential. Within our moms' groups and throughout our lives, we will invite much more joy and freedom if we make it a habit to fan fires, support each other, and celebrate other women doing interesting things in their lives. Together, let's acknowledge that if one of us is held back, we're all held back; however, if one among us is celebrated and encouraged, we all become powerful.

As a group, we can dismantle the culture of scarcity we've built around ourselves. Love is not finite. I love my son Oliver with all my heart, and yet what do I have left for my son Eli and my daughter Sintayehu? More love, of course; it's not a finite commodity! There is love and then there is more love. The same is true in all of our relationships with each other. Your best friend commands a room and exudes charm? Delight in her. Someone else's charm doesn't make you any less charming; it just makes for an even more beautiful and interesting world.

In order to allow our Mama Bears to thrive, we must be intentional within our groups to see the good and celebrate the potential in everyone. There is no limit to greatness.

Challenge #6—Trouble lurks.

A common classroom behavioral strategy is to keep students engaged so they don't have the desire to do anything but the day's lesson. The same is true of household management. For instance, if you know your morning routine breeds stress, you'll do your best to prepare for it. By packing backpacks and lunches before bed, you eliminate the morning panic of not being able to find the right folder or running out of time before it's time to leave.

Just as in the classroom or in your home, you can avoid tense moments within your moms' group by having a general plan in place before trouble comes knocking. Before each new book, study, or project, review your mission statement, vision statement, and values. Review the generalities and make sure that you're living up to your original plan and purpose before you start plugging in specific details.

It is also wise to discuss and decide how to handle conflict within your group before it actually comes up. Not everyone will agree at every moment about what your group should be doing to serve the world. Not everyone will agree on what book you should read together or what Bible study you should complete. Before you roll up your sleeves and dig in, discuss the structure of the group as a whole. Ask yourselves how you will decide what to work on or what to read. Will there be a different leader for each task or season to make final decisions, or will the majority rule with each decision that needs to be made? If there is a designated leader, how often will a new one be called? By putting a plan in place, you will effectively avoid potential sources of dispute.

Though you are not exactly an official organization with 501(c)(3) status, it wouldn't hurt to take yourselves just as seriously. Some might bring business experience to the table, and the group can benefit from this perspective. Perhaps you have a former project manager in your midst. Tap into her insight to garner how best to execute your dreams while still maintaining healthy relationships.

There is no shame in saying that there may come a time when you arrive at a point of conflict that seems unlikely to resolve itself. If this happens, don't be afraid to seek trustworthy help. Rather than allowing the problem to drag out and potentially fracture relationships, involve a third party to help resolve and restore.

When there came a moment of tension within the Church of Wrigleyville moms' group, we invited a pastor to come to a meeting and help us navigate it. What began as an uncomfortable situation brought about by change, an increasing number of mamas, and an increasing significance within the church community ended as a period of growth and maturity for our group. This healthy conflict resolution was imperative and is part of the reason that nearly a decade later relationships continue to grow.

Challenge #7—The critics have their day.

Do you refer to yourself as a stay-at-home mom? Repeat after me: I am not *just* a mom. Seriously, say it out loud. I am not *just* a mom.

I cringe when I hear women hem and haw when asked the common (though in my opinion way overused) get-to-know-you question, "What do you do?"

"Oh, I just stay home with the kids," she replies.

And it's like fingernails on a chalkboard when I hear women say that they don't work. "I don't work. I'm just a stay-at-home mom." You *do* work. And you are not *just* a mom.

Do you refer to yourself as a working mom? Repeat after me: I care about my children. Seriously, say it out loud: I care about my children profoundly and with all of my heart.

Whether you work outside the home by choice, necessity, sheer joy, or calling, it in no way affects your ability to be the mom you were made to be. Without exploring the ever-present cultural mommy wars here, let's just agree that we're all in this together. Women who are employed outside the home are just as invested in their children as those who are the full-time caregivers of their children.

These statements likely reflect your inner critic, and this voice is bothersome for two reasons. First, as humans we are living, breathing, multifaceted beings with unbelievable talents, sincere wants, complex roles, and fantastic desires. Yes, you may be a mom, but you are also a sister, friend, daughter, lover of art or music or yoga, significant other, and living, breathing individual. You are a total of all these different aspects of your existence and then some. Second, describing yourself as "just a mom" devalues the role of motherhood in our society. A mom is perhaps the biggest influencer in a child's life, hence an enormous force in the world at large. Lest we not forget the old, and in my opinion spot-on, adage, "The hand that rocks the cradle is the hand that rules the world."

So let's get over the idea that you don't feel legitimate because you don't earn a paycheck for rearing your children and guiding them throughout their day. Let's release the belief that there is less value in women whose primary work is raising their children. And let's let go of the notion that a mom who works outside the home and doesn't bring homemade cookies to the school bake sale is neglecting her child. Let's say good-bye to the idea that a woman who leaves her home to go to work each day doesn't have enough energy to properly love her son or daughter. Ignore these voices and put them in their place so you are free to do the phenomenal work of mothering your children and ministering to the world.

Unfortunately, you might not be your only critic. There may be others in your world who do not take you as seriously as they otherwise might, simply because you devote your days to shaping the next generation or making positive change in the world. That's their misguided notion, though, not yours. I hope you will learn to ignore the fact that some people might see you and the work your moms' group does as "cute" or "precious"—seemingly innocuous but ultimately degrading adjectives that might draw Mama Bear's claws. We are women who are also mothers who happen to have enormous gifts, talents, energy, and drive. We bring these things to the table, and we organize ourselves in ways that will ultimately make a positive impact on the world. We are not cute or precious; we are strong and powerful. We begin showing this to the world by taking ourselves seriously.

After we start to believe our own worth, we will more likely convince our family members, the leaders in our church, and those in our circles of influence that the work our moms' group is doing is legitimate and worthwhile. By gaining the support of our larger communities, we can allow our enthusiasm to spread, ultimately encouraging others to live their lives for love.

Challenge #8—Things aren't always as they seem.

I'll say it again: you are not a mindless, minivan-driving machine. In fact, the group of you are intelligent, thoughtful women who want to use their gifts for good. With this goal comes the responsibility of research, which you are more than capable of doing.

As you're deciding where your group will spend its precious time and resources, you will need to be thorough in your investigation of the recipient of your gifts. This requires diligence and the absolute refusal to take things at face value. You must dig in and learn about what lies behind your initial promptings. Use your God-given intellect to scour the world for do-good opportunities with integrity. Do not be swayed by slick marketing or the appropriate buzzwords. Let's face it, just because an organization proclaims to be Christian doesn't mean that it is an automatic choice. There are a lot of well-intentioned but poorly run organizations in this world that survive solely because of a Christian label. Don't allow your group to be a victim of faulty labels and slick marketing. Dig in and look for quality. Strive for what is good and pure and excellent. If you find yourselves leaning toward a particular project, group, or need, become an expert in the matter and choose your strategy for helping wisely.

Such shrewdness is biblical. In Matthew, Jesus instructs his followers: "Do not give dogs what is sacred; do not throw your pearls to pigs" (7:6). I don't think God gives up on any of us who are working for good, but we still must choose wisely, capturing what's best at that particular moment in time. This is especially true when you are trying to raise awareness or raise funds. If you're trumpeting a cause or raising money, it's imperative that you research the organization you're working with. Ask difficult questions and investigate thoroughly. If you are selling a product, question how the product is produced. If you are lending a hand to a group, know what the group stands for and then decide how best to help, or whether or not to take action at that particular moment.

When I first started working in rural, underresourced areas in Tanzania, I listened to a story of good intentions told as a cautionary tale. A group of big-hearted women from the United States learned that a hospital in the mountains of rural Tanzania did not have bassinettes to put next to maternity-ward beds so that the new mothers could place their babies down for naps while they themselves rested. The women from the United States worked hard and raised enough money to send a shipment of sturdy bassinettes to East Africa. Later, they inquired whether or not the bassinettes were appreciated and being used. The bassinettes were being used, they learned, but not in the way that the group had anticipated. The new, local moms who delivered at the Tanzanian hospital weren't using the bassinettes for their babies. Why would they? They constantly wore their babies close to their bodies tucked within vibrantly printed wraps, rarely setting them down. However, they found that the sturdy bassinettes on casters made fabulous laundry carts.

We are experienced sleuths and decision-makers. We dig online for product reviews of everything from car seats to strollers to BPA-free bottles to bikes; we interview older and wiser parents regarding their in-the-trenches experiences; and we read books, join forums, and listen to podcasts on parenting techniques. We strive to educate ourselves and then choose what we believe to be best. This should also be true of your social-action efforts. Err on the side of love, but don't let love blind you. Be smart when you spend yourself.

C. S. Lewis writes about this sort of engagement in his book *Mere Christianity*, reminding the reader that Jesus tells us to be not only "as harmless as doves," but also "as wise as serpents." Lewis writes,

> God wants a child's heart, but a grown-up's head. He wants us to be simple, single-minded, affectionate, and teachable, as good children are; but He also wants every bit of intelligence we have to be alert at its job, and in first-class fighting trim. The fact that you are giving money to a charity does not mean that you need not try to find out whether that charity is a fraud or not.[5]

It's likely that as your ministry blooms, you'll want to share your joy and passion with others. Your careful research will allow you to speak confidently about the work you're doing.

Challenge #9—Fear paralyzes.

Fear can be paralyzing. There is, of course, a healthy fear that God has given to us that works in preservation of our human selves. However, we pick up a lot of unhealthy fear by living in the place and time that we do, and from simply being human. Many times throughout my life, I have missed opportunities for growth and joy simply because I was afraid. Afraid of what others might think, afraid I might look foolish, afraid I didn't have the right outfit, afraid of how much money I would have to part with, afraid I might fail. However, 1 John 4:18 says that God's love drives out fear. Being mindful of God's unending love will eradicate all fear and doubt. I take great comfort in knowing that no matter what, God's love for me—and for you—does not end.

And so what if you fail? What if you can't find enough people to donate items of clothing to fill the closet at the women's shelter? What if the teenage mothers you planned a brunch for just sit on the other side of the room and do not act all that interested in interacting with you? What if no one buys the jewelry you made and marketed and hoped to sell in order to benefit the food pantry? What if you aren't actually able to send ten thousand antimalarial nets to Nigeria as you'd audaciously hoped? What if you find yourselves dealing with disappointment?

Teddy Roosevelt provides a forceful answer that, for a moment, we'll pretend he directed at a woman rather than a man:

> It is not the critic who counts; not the woman who
> points out how the strong woman stumbles, or where
> the doer of deeds could have done them better. The
> credit belongs to the woman who is actually in the arena,
> whose face is marred by dust and sweat and blood;
> who strives valiantly; who errs, who comes short again
> and again, because there is no effort without error and

shortcoming; but who does actually strive to do the deeds; who knows great enthusiasms, the great devotions; who spends herself in a worthy cause; who at the best knows in the end the triumph of high achievement, and who at the worst, if she fails, at least fails while daring greatly, so that her place shall never be with those cold and timid souls who neither know victory nor defeat.[6]

Ladies, if you don't throw your hat into the ring, how will you know what your moms' group is capable of? Take note: you are not cold or timid souls. You are willing to spend yourselves on a worthy cause, and you have girlfriends and a God who have your back. You dream big and work hard. You hold the power of Mama Bear within. You continue to engage the battle with Supermom, and you keep winning and getting stronger and stronger. Let your imaginations run wild and then roll up your sleeves. Dream big and bold and dusty dreams. Together, your moms' group—with its tremendous force of mother love—is capable of amazing things. Let no one convince you otherwise.

· ·

NOTES

[1]Brennan Manning, *Abba's Child: The Cry of the Heart for Intimate Belonging* (Colorado Springs: NavPress, 2015), 140.

[2]Hilary Stour, "Frazzled Moms Push Back Against Volunteering," *New York Times,* December 1, 2010, accessed July 19, 2016, http://www.nytimes.com/2010/12/02/garden/02parents.html.

[3]Joan Chittister, *Wisdom Distilled from the Daily: Living the Rule of St. Benedict Today* (New York: HarperCollins, 1991), 11.

[4]Melena Ryzik, "Amy Poehler and Tina Fey: When Leaning In, Laughing Matters," *New York Times,* December 3, 2015, accessed July 20, 2016, http://

www.nytimes.com/2015/12/06/movies/amy-poehler-and-tina-fey-when
-leaning-in-laughing-matters.html.

[5]C. S. Lewis, *Mere Christianity* (New York: HarperOne, 2001), 77.

[6]Theodore Roosevelt, "Citizenship in a Republic" (speech given at the Sorbonne in Paris, France, April 23, 1910). Quote was modified to speak of women rather than men.

CHAPTER ELEVEN

Wondrous Waves

I was thirsty and you gave me something to drink.
—Matthew 25:35

Down by the banks of the muddy Mississippi River in the stretch of the Midwest where Illinois and Iowa are divided by the imposing water, you'll find clay-colored bluffs, lush prairie, and miles and miles of rolling hills. On stormy days, the river is restless and the waves harsh. When the sun shines, you can't help but delight in the calm of the gentle blue water and the countryside painted by the pop of golden black-eyed Susans and dark-pink coneflowers. During the summer months, pleasant country roads encased by wildflowers growing in deep ditches color the monotony of cornfields. The fall brings vibrant colors, luscious apple orchards, and evidence of harvest all around. Each season is clearly defined. Summers are hot and humid; winters are icy and frigid. Amid the Midwest landscape—up and down the Mississippi—you don't have to look too hard to find small cities and tiny river towns filled with churches, cafes, and remarkable characters.

After months of deliberation, my husband and I, along with our two young sons, relocated from Roscoe Village, a busy neighborhood on the north side of Chicago, to a city next to the Mississippi River three hours away. We moved from the place that, in our young married life, we had grown to love to the place that, as native Iowans, we both loved as children. A lot of this had to do with our young sons and the pending arrival of our daughter. We wanted our children to grow up surrounded by cousins, grandparents, aunts, and uncles (most of whom live in this area), and we were starting to itch for a certain ease of life that we knew Iowa would offer.

For years we had anticipated growing out of our tiny Chicago apartment and ultimately started to get anxious about feeling settled. So we lined up some interviews, packed some boxes, rented a truck, and headed west to our new city along the mighty river. Our return to our roots surprised many of our friends, but the move felt natural to my husband and me. We were looking for a place to spread out and raise our family, and what one might assume to be a sleepy set of small cities along a powerful river has proven itself to be more than that over and over again.

We said a long and painful good-bye to our friends and our beloved city and found ourselves settling into a land of little traffic and free and ample parking. Though I missed our friends and our old city life, I happily greeted the convenience and ease that I found here. This I expected.

What I didn't expect, however, and couldn't have begun to predict, was that shortly after moving away from my bustling city, our community of friends, and my Wrigleyville moms' group, I would be swept into a social movement led by a group of fierce Midwestern mamas. In a city along the Mississippi with nary a Starbucks in sight, a grassroots movement began that has resulted in beautiful relationships, personal fulfillment, remarkable memories, great excitement, and nearly half a million dollars for clean-water wells throughout the world.

........................❤........................

It began with a group of four Mama Bears. Jody Landers, Amy Smith, Cassie Burback, and Tesi Klipsch (my sister-in-law—the two of us married a pair of handsome brothers within just months of one another) met at their church in Muscatine, Iowa, a picturesque city of twenty-three thousand people perched right on the banks of the Mississippi. Their goal was to work on social-justice projects within their community. At the time, these women were primarily stay-at-home mothers with seventeen children among them.

Take a moment to imagine their gatherings. Though they met on Sundays without children in tow, the work they did throughout the week often included moms in yoga pants armed with laptops, Goldfish, and a lot of coffee. A dozen or so preschool-aged children whirled around them as this group of determined women planned their grand philanthropic adventures. They were women, guided by God and a common goal, making the most of the situation in which they found themselves.

These are the women I mentioned earlier in the book who raised money for Plumpy'Nut and gathered backpacks filled with essentials for the local Department of Children and Human Services. After the success of these endeavors, they found themselves with bolstered confidence and an amped-up urgency to serve the world around them. They were on fire with the presence of God in their lives, with the relationships they were building with one another, and with the tangible good they were able to do around them. They felt fulfilled by being the hands and feet of Christ and were amused by the way God had used them.

At the end of the hot and humid summer of 2009, the group began to discuss a new project. They brainstormed and dreamed and researched, finding that they kept coming back to the world water crisis. They learned that at that time, one in six people worldwide[1] did not have access to clean water. They learned that people without access to clean water gather dirty water from the same source that their animals drink from and their dirty clothes are washed in. Parasites in this water make them sick, and often kill them. Women are attacked and raped on the long journey to a water source—assuming there is a source available. Sometimes children are kept out of school to gather the families' water. As mothers, the four were amazed and heartbroken: 4,500 children died each day as a result of the lack of clean water.

From their comfortable lives in eastern Iowa, right along the flowing water of the mighty Mississippi River, an even deeper chord was struck for this group of moms. They learned that many Africans in particular live without clean water. This made a huge impression on all of the women, but especially on Jody, who had adopted twins from Sierra Leone just months before, and Tesi, whose middle child had been adopted from Ethiopia the previous spring. The reality of this crisis was unfathomable to this group of Mama Bears. Little more than geography separated those children dying from lack of clean water from their own.

The small group of women dug in and conducted extensive research. In doing so, what began with heartbreak and hopelessness turned into joy and vigor. This worldwide lack of safe drinking water could conceivably be remedied. In fact, they found that in their own lifetimes, the entire world could gain access to clean water. The technology was there—and so was the water, just below the surface in many parts of the world—and it was mostly a matter of education, tools, and resources.

As they researched and read and discussed and watched documentaries, the group discovered something else that shocked them. It's estimated that Americans spend $457 billion each Christmas. The World Bank estimates the cost of reaching "basic levels of coverage . . . in water and sanitation" to be $9 billion to $30 billion for a year for "achieving universal coverage" for water and sanitation. The same report says that taking the estimates and the caveats together, the estimated cost for providing basic levels of coverage universally is between $5 billion and $21 billion.[2]

With this bit of information, the women grew angry. They allowed themselves to feel this anger and to let it fester. They asked incredulous questions aloud to one another. They spat words of disbelief. Their Mama Bears started to growl.

Several months before Christmas, they decided that they would use this information and their anger and their energy and their love of Christ and their sphere of influence, and they would try to raise $5,000—enough to build one freshwater well in a village that was without a clean-water source. They dreamed about convincing everyone they knew to give part of their Christmas cash to clean-water solutions, making the world a better place for a group of brothers and sisters (and mothers, in particular) who were suffering a world away. They trusted God, they knew their community, and they had the audacity to believe that with a little encouragement and hard work, their ministry could provide a much-needed solution.

The women decided to raise their funds for an organization named charity: water. They did their homework and had great confidence in charity: water, partly because it had private donors who funded all of the overhead costs, making it possible for 100 percent of the donations coming from individuals to go directly to freshwater projects. At the time, charity: water estimated that a donation of twenty dollars would give one person access to clean, fresh water for twenty years.

Twenty dollars. Twenty years. They knew this was something they could get behind. These Midwestern moms had intense anger that turned into passion and a great hope that they could do something tangible to make the world a better place. They prayed. They planned. They found the time to roll up their sleeves and get to work. This group of moms hoped to turn the tides of consumerism to compassion and ask people to consider giving "water" for Christmas to their loved ones. They were bolstered by the strength of friendship and were free to take a good look at their individual gifts and passions. They used their collective talents and greatest joys and went to work for the least of these.

Just before the holiday season, in a small city next to a great big river, a group of moms had a passion, a prayer, and a solid plan. They named their campaign "Water for Christmas" and a small, grassroots, Mama Bear-led revolution was born.

· ❤ ·

What unfolded next was remarkable. It was as if floodgates opened and anyone associated with these inspiring women couldn't help but jump onto the ship and ride the waves of positive change.

Amy, who is a gifted artist and mother of five children, began designing jewelry and selling it for the cause. She chose beautiful blue beads and leather bands and designed the first of many "Water for Christmas" bracelets. At five dollars a pop (100 percent of the purchase went to charity: water), they sold like hotcakes, and she soon found her fingers fatigued just trying to keep up with the demand. Her great joy was put to work for the kingdom of God.

Amy's mother, Barbara Bullock, is also an artist. When she caught wind of the clean-water well that her daughter and friends were trying to build, she jumped in and designed a stained-glass

Christmas ornament in the shape of a clear water droplet. Again, it seemed that everyone who saw the ornament wanted one to hang on their Christmas tree or on the window above their kitchen sink. Every dollar she earned was contributed directly to her daughter's dream and the proven work of charity: water.

These women donated their time, talent, and materials for the benefit of those who were thirsty. Each took something she loved (creating beauty with her hands) and used her passion for good. They embody the words of the mystic poet Rumi: "In your light I learn how to love. In your beauty, how to make poems. You dance inside my chest where no one sees you, but sometimes I do, and that sight becomes this art."

The experience changed Amy's life. Not only does she now have the Water for Christmas logo tattooed on her wrist, but since the time Water for Christmas was launched, she has fallen in love with a new continent. Amy and her husband, Steve, added to their brood of five children by adopting a sixth, a young girl named Bosena, from Ethiopia in 2010. Shortly after that, Amy turned her experiences into a new venture. She and another woman founded their own nonprofit: Because Every Mother Matters (BEMM). BEMM works in Ethiopia to help mothers find dignity by connecting resources here in the States to opportunities for impoverished women where her daughter was born. From her home base of Muscatine, Iowa, Amy has engaged with the least of these throughout the world.

A mother of three and trained classroom teacher, Cassie created ingenious and impactful lesson plans and shared with elementary classroom teachers. Soon, rooms full of engaged children learned about the lack of such a basic human need and joyfully got involved. She leveraged her popular family blog to spread the word about Water for Christmas. Children throughout the country listened to their teachers talk about water and then they gathered their change, held bake sales, and ran lemonade stands to raise money.

Blogs and social media played a huge role in this savvy Mama Bear group's fight for justice. Jody, who became the driving force and voice of the movement, used the power of social networking to grow the cause. Her widely read blog became the hub of the work being done. She posted about water and invited her readers from all over the country to join the movement. People read her impassioned words and responded. Soon she was being linked to hundreds of other bloggers, and stories of people (primarily mothers) throughout the country came pouring in with ways in which they, too, were raising money for Water for Christmas. Her great wisdom, incredible gift of writing, and smart use of social networking inspired countless people and changed hearts and lives. The grassroots movement grew.

Jody and the group also used Facebook as a mobilizing force. With the help of a FB friend in New Zealand, "Facebook Fridays" ultimately raised over $10,000 for Water for Christmas. Hundreds of people "friended" the cause and willingly gave ten dollars every Friday in an act of communal generosity. At that time, Jody had a set of two-year-old twins and two preschoolers at home and two older children in elementary school. During this period in her life, she clearly wasn't able to make social change from a corporate office building or even a church office. I can promise you that she did not strap on a pair of heels at any point during the Water for Christmas campaign. But she did move mountains from her laptop at home.

Tesi, a former marketing professional, used her marketing know-how to further the vision. Tesi laughingly told her friends that she didn't have the skills to create a spreadsheet or make a bracelet, but she could use her communications degree, her interest in cinematography, and her public relations prowess to garner attention for the movement. What she did was indeed very creative:

she danced for water. She powered up her iPod and dared to dance on a sunny day with a midwestern background as her husband rolled the camera. Next, she posted the edited video of herself dancing to the Black Eyed Peas on YouTube. After posting the video (and linking it to her blog and Facebook), she asked her readers and friends to take a moment to watch what she was willing to do for clean water. Before they watched the video, she invited the curious viewers to click on a link and donate to Water for Christmas as a sort of viewing fee. She then invited others to dance for water and post it online for their friends to see, raising both money and awareness.

And dance they did. How could you not? After hearing my sister-in-law's vision and passion, I couldn't possibly say no to her request to dance for water. I powered up U2's "Vertigo" (on *How to Dismantle an Atomic Bomb*) and danced joyfully around in an empty swimming pool in the middle of eastern Iowa. (Very theatrical and symbolic, you see.) Disregarding any possible teasing from my friends and family, I danced like I'd never danced before. As a dramatic finish, I allowed Tesi to dump a bucket of water over my head as the music faded and the camera rolled. (Believe it or not, this was long before the Ice Bucket Challenge of 2015.) My two children, as well as my niece and nephew, watched the whole thing and were absolutely tickled by the sight of two adults doing something that adults don't typically do. Our children later begged to dance for water and saved their own coins for the cause as well. Tesi recorded me dancing, my brother-in-law edited the footage, and we posted it on YouTube, alerting friends to our passion via blogs and social media. I then sent an email asking everyone I had ever met to watch my growing passion and to give money to Water for Christmas. Dozens of people danced, even more gave money, and soon we were hearing all kinds of stories of friends, family, and long-lost acquaintances being bitten by the bug to help others in big and small ways.

With the use of blogs and Facebook, the movement grew quickly. Moms all over the country joined forces and used their social platforms to promote Water for Christmas. Link upon link told the story of this group of passionate, creative mamas. People trumpeted their own efforts online and the word spread far and wide.

One junior high school in a neighboring community heard about charity: water—and the passion that this group of local moms had planted—through a friend who was connected to the group. Jessie Bishop, a part-time social studies teacher with two young children of her own, made sure every single student at the junior high where she taught learned about the world water crisis and what they could do to help. What resulted was over $1,000 dollars raised for Water for Christmas.

A group of her fashion-loving students designed T-shirts, had them printed, and sold them to their classmates, giving their profits to Water for Christmas. The eighth grade class hosted a dance, with the admission fee being a donation to the cause. Their heroic teachers saw the light in the students' eyes and agreed to have whipped-cream pies thrown in their faces and eggs broken over their heads for a dollar a shot. Another teacher set up a video-game console and asked for a dollar per turn. The teachers recognized the potential their students—many of whom came from impoverished homes themselves and found doing good for others to be incredibly empowering—had and took advantage of the energy and interest they had developed for the world water crisis.

At another local junior high school, Tom Randleman, a teacher and member of the Muscatine church, heard about the splash and enlisted high school students to help. Students made and sold bracelets and T-shirts for Water for Christmas. Eventually, these students did their own research and set a goal of raising $20,000 to provide a well not only for an entire village, but also to provide a school with access to clean water.

In just a couple of months, the ripples moved on and on. Jody's sister-in-law (a mother of two young girls) developed a website from her California home that helped educate others and encourage them to launch their own creative ways to get involved and raise money. Another pair of local women used their passion for running to raise money and awareness for water. The two of them planned and held a road race right along the banks of the Mississippi River. Because of their hard work and enthusiasm, on one crisp, sunny October morning, $4,000 was raised for charity: water. They planned, promoted, and held the race yearly for the next two years, raising enough money to change the lives of hundreds of people across the ocean and providing local individuals and families an excuse to spend a fall morning outside.

Of course, not everyone is a runner or blogger or dancer. No matter. When crafters caught the Water for Christmas bug and decided to use their love of art and handiwork, the movement flourished further. Eventually, Cassie set up a Water for Christmas Etsy shop to which people from all over the country (again, mostly mothers) donated their handiwork. One group of women spent a weekend at a crafting "retreat" of sorts. They gathered together in one woman's home with sewing machines, good food, and a few bottles of wine, and together they created countless appliqued T-shirts, bracelets, and accessories to stock the Etsy shop. Back in Muscatine, Cassie turned her dining room into a makeshift post office and diligently filled orders as they came pouring in. In one season alone, the Water for Christmas Etsy shop raised $10,000. Lives changed, one handmade Christmas gift at a time.

When artist Sheila Mesick heard about what the group of local women were trying to do, she created a piece of art to be auctioned off for Water for Christmas. In doing so, she raised enough money to give five people access to fresh water for twenty years. She took her love of mankind and her talent and love of painting and joined the movement. So did Dana Linze-Dengler. And Jen VanOort. And Anna Pate. And Ann Hartley. These women—and many, many more—took their love of mankind and their talent in painting and creating and joined the movement. Another friend named Sara donated a quilt she made. And Sarah the poet? Well, she donated a lovely, hand-stamped broadside of an original poem that she wrote about wind and water and it, too, was auctioned off for the cause. People like these women witnessed a bit of passion and were moved to explore it on their own, each adding their unique voices to the raging waves of change.

There are many other stories just like these that came out of this remarkable movement, all because of the audacity and passion of a group of stay-at-home moms with a hand on the Bible, a pulse on the world, a strong community, and a bit of creative vision. They were moms on the move. They were Mama Bears who channeled their anger and turned it into beauty. Within just a few months of the Water for Christmas campaign, the community of givers raised $65,000—well beyond the $5,000 the group had originally hoped for.

With all of the donations from Iowa pouring in, the people in the offices of charity: water in New York City began to notice and wonder what was going on. They had helped set up a fundraising page so that people could donate online and were amused by the creative YouTube dances being posted each day. They wanted to learn more about the people involved in such enthusiastic fundraising. What was it that made these moms from the Midwest so convincing?

The president of charity: water, Scott Harrison, decided to head west for a weekend to meet the moms and help further cast the vision to the community. When they heard he was coming, the team (now made up of over two dozen people) really started turning their wheels. Fundraising parties were planned for both Muscatine and just up the river in Davenport. Churches and other public venues were booked for community lectures. Schools held assemblies. The press was alerted. Harrison attended thirteen different events over the course of four days. The number of wells being built grew beyond everyone's expectation.

What had begun as the hope of four moms building one well before Christmas 2009 turned into hundreds of people waking up to injustice and taking tangible measures to create change. As of August 2016, Water for Christmas has raised over a half million dollars in order to provide clean, fresh water sources for people who were once without. Just last year, $36,000 was raised at the Water Party, the Saturday event that began as part of the Water for Christmas movement and now draws over four hundred people. The party alone, now approaching its eighth year and still mom organized and mom implemented, has raised well over $100,000 for clean water solutions in Liberia, Uganda, India, and Tanzania.

For me, the whole experience felt like an outrageous answer to prayer. As I was searching for a new community of God-loving women after making a new home for our family, I found a group that freely used their love of God and channeled it into loving the world. In the most beautiful, fulfilling way, I was carried away by the tides of change that these women had created and that God was sustaining.

The prayers that I began praying over the years with my Chicago moms' group were answered in an unexpected way. It didn't take long for me to become hooked on the energy and vision of these women. New in town, I did my own personal research and then joined the Water for Christmas team. I went on to contribute in ways that brought me personal joy and wonder. The Holy Spirit was at work in a way that made us feel very much alive and part of this world.

Not only did I look forward to the purposeful fellowship I enjoyed with these women, but I found myself lying awake at night composing the perfect Water for Christmas press release in my mind. I kept a notebook next to my bed to record ideas for fund-raising events. I woke up with bags under my eyes, not able to sleep from all of the excitement, and yet I was energized. I often thought of Lamentations 2:19 as my mind raced and my heart fluttered with passion. "Arise, cry out in the night, as the watches of the night begin; pour out your heart like water in the presence of the Lord. Lift up your hands to him for the lives of your children, who faint from hunger at every street corner."

God's presence was like a mighty flood. During a time of change, adjustment, and a whole lot of sadness stemming from missing my friends and life in Chicago, God provided opportunities for new friendship and magnificent growth.

All the people who invested in the dream of Water for Christmas were much like the women who spearheaded the movement—individuals with hearts for justice. This was not a movement of large contributions. There were no large corporations backing the efforts of this small group of people. Rather, it only happened because a whole lot of little people put their five, ten, and twenty dollar bills together for something bigger than themselves. People who read Facebook status updates on Friday and decided to forgo lunch out and instead put the cash toward a clean-water solution. People who took a hard look at their purchasing power and decided to use it for good. It was teachers engaging students and couples holding late-night conversations about giving. Many of us found ourselves indebted to a bold example of what it might look like when a small group of people gathers together to love God and love the world.

There is no doubt that both here in the Upper Mississippi region and beyond, the waves of change that these moms helped inspire roll on and on and on.

It's as Jody told the *Huffington Post* a few years later, after she had moved to Washington state and turned her attention to cofounding a nonprofit organization called The Adventure Project. "Each of our children has added profound value to our lives," she said of her family and her experience. "And I do believe that there is a fierceness to a mother's love that cannot be reproduced. And I think I realized that there is something universal about that. Supporting this campaign is an opportunity to live beyond those diapers, and Legos, and homework, and baseball practices and touch the lives of women we've never met."[3]

My perspective of what is possible changed after meeting this group of moms and witnessing the Water for Christmas experience. I had the chance to see firsthand the impact that could be made by a group of committed individuals who prayed together and dared to dream. None of them worked out of sleek offices or had access to huge bank accounts. Quite the opposite, in fact. Water for Christmas was a grassroots movement started by Mama Bears who worked out of living rooms littered with Power Rangers and Fisher Price gadgets. They were responsible for packing lunches, getting children to school on time, and doing the many, many things that small, dependent people require. Some worked outside of the home. Some made motherhood their full-time vocation. All of them passionately loved their children completely and then mustered up the strength and energy to love their neighbors as well. They turned their mom-of-young-children circumstances into joyful witness. They fell into bed exhausted. They had passion and friendship and the presence of a God who loves them.

When it comes down to it, we all have access to that. The question is: How might we use it?

NOTES

[1]Thanks to the amazing work that has been done by dozens of effective aid organizations since 2009, the number is now estimated to be one in seven people.

[2]www.water.cc.

[3]Nicole Skibola, "Wife, Mother, Social Impact Trailblazer: Bridging the World of Social Change," *The Huffington Post*, October 13, 2011, accessed June 28, 2016, http://www.huffingtonpost.com/nicole-skibola/the-adventure-project _b_1005982.html.

CHAPTER TWELVE

Into the Wild

The best thing to do with the best things of life
is to give them away.
—Doris Day

Every time I travel to East Africa—to Tanzania for the NGO I work for or to Ethiopia where we adopted our third child—I become convinced that every mom that I have ever met needs to board the next plane and spend a week learning and growing. I want to send out an email planting the seed. *We need to leave right now,* I think. *Every last one of us needs to drop everything, buy a ticket, pack a bag, and run (not walk) out the door.*

I imagine the transformative power of travel and the fun we would all have together exploring a new country and continent, observing both what's beautiful and what's broken. I envision Jen planning our meals and managing our time. I see Sara learning all she can about the deep sense of community that exists and the lack of health care and economic opportunity, and then coming back to the United States and amplifying the voices of the marginalized from her pulpit at the church where she preaches. I see Tesi rising early each morning for her daily yoga practice and coming back refreshed and full of wisdom. I picture Holly in all her sweetness and her affection soaking up the children we may meet. What joy we would find in exploring a new culture together! What great conversations we could have while learning about the progress of women working in their own unique ways to make their world better! To me, the plan shapes up to be incredibly sound.

And then, I suppose, reality sets in. Though I still secretly hope that one day my beloved mom-friends will travel together and spend a week exploring, supporting sustainable projects, and learning about a new culture, I eventually realize that now is probably not the right time to make the journey. Last-minute tickets don't come cheap. At present, we all have young children at home to mind, and spending time away from our families and responsibilities will feel more kosher when our little people are more independent and don't rely quite so much on our care. Plus, I realize we might not actually need to be so dramatic in order to make a difference. As Mother Teresa wisely stated, "Calcuttas are everywhere if only we have eyes to see. Find your Calcutta."

Still, those initial promptings are strong, and I continue to try to figure out what they might mean in my life. Several of my friends and I live in a neighborhood with a hospital that houses a Neonatal Intensive Care Unit. Might God be leading us to rock babies and provide comfort there? Or perhaps to take an hour out of the day, walk to a local nursing home, and read aloud to the residents? Maybe.

And yet I wonder if this initial nudge, which prompts me to dream aloud about a transformative journey, is from the Holy Spirit. How is God asking us to respond? Is this a message for me personally, or am I meant to drag other moms into it?

I'm not sure that it's ever *easy* to discern God's will in our lives, and as a group of Mama Bears, we might find ourselves navigating uncharted wilderness together as we decide how best to spring to action. Because of this, I am convinced that positioning yourself in the presence of God is the place to start. Whether we feel God's presence while taking quiet walks, sitting at a coffee shop writing in a journal, or during formal worship at church, we each need to seek God and engage in conversation about what he might have in store for us as individuals, as well as fired-up moms. I also believe we need to use our reserves. If you've got a whole group of women who want to lift you up, let them lift you up and help you decipher God's will in your life, both as an individual and as part of a community. Prayer is a necessary part of discernment, and we are wise to engage in communal prayer seeking God's loving presence and guidance.

When it comes to the adventure of discernment, I love the perspective of Sister Rose Mary Dougherty who writes in her book *Group Spiritual Direction* that seeking God's direction for our lives is often "equated with a skill which we must master rather than the gift of God's love which guides us home to love."[1] We may feel like we're out in the wild, but when we're seeking God, his will always guides us home to love. So often I busy myself searching for clues and cryptic messages from God and forget how much he loves me and wants me to enjoy his love and this life. I get so caught up in doing the *right* thing as if my life depended on it that I forget that what God has for me is good, that his guidance is toward love, and that his will is not always a concrete path leading in one specific direction. In other words, there may be more than one answer. We can be assured as we discern God's will that Mama Bear, no matter her master plan, is walking toward love.

Like any good teacher will tell you, reflection is necessary. As you seek God's presence and inquire about the path your group should take, be prayerful and reflective. Encourage a collective attitude of yearning to live out love in your life. Even if you don't hear a definitive answer or feel a sense of direction, exercise trust in our good and gracious God. As Dougherty says,

> We can never know all there is of any given circumstance. And the truth often transcends the obvious. There comes a time when we are invited into simple faith as we make decisions, trusting God to transform the ambiguity of our hearts with the fire of love and to be with us in and through the uncertainty. . . . Our task is to live into the decision seeking the support of others who share our desire for God. Gradually we come to *live in a place of love and allow that love to lead.*[2]

This trust in God is a posture from which to love one another and the world around us. We practice and will make mistakes, but we benefit from our grace-giving community who does everything with love.

When describing my faith to others, I often refer to the God I serve as "Love-with-a-Capital-L." Love incarnate. A yummy Love that grants peace when I'm troubled.[3] A steady, all-encompassing Love that has no borders and knows no bounds.

This Love is a source of strength that propels me forward. It bends toward beauty and it always errs on the side of acceptance, forgiveness, and the celebration of the diversity and depth of our humanity. It's this Love and the kindness shown to me by others that makes me want to cry out to others, "Come look! Let me show you how good this is! Come and see!"[4]

As Mama Bears, we can bathe in this love. We can create a community set on carefully observing what unfolds as we walk through life. In what ways does Love instruct us? How do we turn our anger into love? How do we make it actionable on earth? Are projects in progress hitting roadblocks and is the frustration level high? Are we at peace with these challenges, or are the burdens too fraught with unsettling anxiety to be worth forging on? Is the plan for action challenging but grounded in the strong desire that it's worth fighting for? We can ask these questions and keep the dialogue alive, realizing that everything will resolve in Love.

Deep down, that's what our Mama Bear inclinations are a powerful response to. When we are even just slightly sure of these beams of love,[5] we can see the potential for redemption all around us. We don't open our eyes to the suffering present in the world and then allow our anger to paralyze us because we can only see what's *troubling* God's creation. We don't engage in loving-kindness because of fear or obligation. There's no fun in that. Rather, we offer a vibrant response of care and service because life is 100 percent better when we do. As we acknowledge how tangible and outrageous God's love is for us, we've got nothing else to do but say thank you and be propelled forward to share that love with others.

This is the response that Mama Bear is made for. As Henri Nouwen wrote, we often speak of love as a feeling. And this feeling of love, it's beautiful and life-giving, he says, but the rich and meaningful lives we crave cannot be based on just a nice feeling. "To love is to think, speak, and act according to the spiritual knowledge that we are infinitely loved by God and called to make that love visible in this world."[6] For as sweet and patient as you might be with your children, and for all the gentleness you bring to your babies, I don't imagine that your Mama Bear is terribly touchy-feely. She's powerful and she's forceful and, depending on how old her children are, she's possibly a tad bit sleep deprived, which gives her the perfect edge. Right now, she's poised to make this love visible in bold strides and helping hands. Her response to love is not passive and it's not a simple *feeling*, as beautiful as that thought might be. By now you know Mama Bear's response is made up of power and action.

And that's exactly what justice worker Gary Haugen asks of us. Borrowing from Friedrich Nietzche, who wrote in *Beyond Good and Evil* that a life worth living requires "a long obedience in the same direction," Haugen states that "the victims of injustice in our world do not need our spasms of passion; they need our long obedience in the same direction—our legs and lungs of endurance; and we need sturdy stores of joy." Precisely what a group of trained Mama Bears, armed with love and a committed community ripe with a mother's love, has to offer.

Examples of long roads toward justice are everywhere. Long and often very bumpy, these paths are interesting to examine. One that I thought about in particular this year was the celebration of Earth Day. For years we've planted trees and we've recycled, upcycled, reused, reduced, and shopped for sustainably harvested products, and yet the headlines are more terrifying today than they were in 1970 when Americans first organized to rally for a cleaner earth. When I realized that the idea of Earth Day had in fact been in existence for longer than I have, it made me feel a little sad. A lifetime of work and yet the unrelenting news cycle of environmental woe left me feeling overwhelmed and helpless to do anything at all. Why ride a bike around town when the polar ice caps are melting rapidly anyway? Why walk the path when so little progress seems to have been made? The same thing could be said of humanitarian efforts. Why, as of 2014, are there still more than fifteen million hungry children in the United States?[7] And when faced with such a staggering number, how can we even dream to help make a dent?

At least, when I'm honest, that's how I feel. Like many among us, I am morally distressed, yet I sometimes feel powerless to respond in a meaningful way. You may have noticed in your own experience that it's a short walk from outrage to numbness.

Those caring for elderly or sick loved ones or who work in helping professions such as health care or social work or education sometimes suffer from compassion fatigue, and experience a gradual emotional numbness. This fatigue stems from exposure to traumatic events or stressful situations and can leave caretakers overwhelmed, exhausted, and unable to implement proper self-care. In a culture where we are constantly exposed to vivid images and a news cycle that never stops, the average citizen—or group of citizens working together for positive change—can feel this weight as well.

Some explain this with the Buddhist idea that sorrow is a "near enemy" of compassion. Being compassionate involves understanding the suffering of another without feeling sorrow or pity. When sorrow surfaces, compassion can turn into unhappiness. Pity can paralyze effort because feeling the emotional pain of another doesn't relieve suffering; it can actually add to it.

Around Earth Day 2016, I heard about Joan Halifax, a Zen abbot and medical anthropologist, who speaks of "empathic distress" and believes that we must stabilize ourselves when we're exposed to suffering. In doing so, she says, we can face the world with more buoyancy, resilience, and hope. During a podcast with Krista Tippett, Roshi Halifax issued a call to action, saying, "The more aware we become, the more responsible we recognize we are for what is and what will be."[8] At the most primal level, my Mama Bear nods her head vigorously. I find Roshi Halifax's words inspiring, but I am left with a practical question: How do I overcome sorrow, steady myself, and proceed with compassion when faced with suffering?

Different people come to this revelation from different places. I do not spend forty hours a week working for a church or organization devoted to fighting hunger or injustice. Nor am I a psychologist or social worker on the frontlines of the violent or unfathomable. However, I am a woman who—with access to clean water, health care, nourishing food, shelter, and a stable environment—has won the lottery in life. So have my friends. In fact, we're undoubtedly a lot like you: people with a recognized privilege, a sense of social responsibility, and an ache to practice compassion in action. I don't want to be paralyzed by bad news; I want to be primed and ready to seek the truth of change. I want to feel the deep press of suffering, to let it resonate, yet to maintain a healthy insight that allows me to separate myself as an individual being.

This can be actualized through the basics: community, self-reflection, meditation, and prayer. But there's something else I've noticed as well. When those on the front lines get tired, they review impact stories. When journalists try to arouse interest and awareness, they tell stories from the field. When Jesus expressed love and virtue in hopes that the masses might understand, he did so through parables. Human beings quiet themselves and listen to stories in order to connect and to awaken our hearts and our consciences.

This is why I pray that tomorrow, when faced with a headline from far away or a struggle on my own street, I'll chase away apathy by listening to the story as it unfolds in front of me. I pray that next I'll summon stillness within the hurry of my life and muster enough perspective to look at my own story. I pray that with clear eyes I'll consider the arc of my life and the kind of character I aspire to be. I'll ask myself, "What decision would make this more interesting? What action aligns with the character I want to be?" Writer Donald Miller believes this posture leads to a new way of responding to the world. "Great characters in exciting stories don't sit around on the couch playing it safe," he writes. "They get up, move, try, fail and risk it all again. Living a great story costs something. People who live great stories know failure isn't a judgment, it's an education."[9]

A group of us gathered over Mother's Day weekend to celebrate at a pretty fabulous "pretend" shower. It didn't look like most baby or bridal showers I've attended, though. In fact, there was not a pregnant mama or bride-to-be in sight. Instead, there was a representative from a local women's shelter there to gather the lavish gifts we had purchased and wrapped prettily and to tell us why the work of the shelter matters in our community. Beth, the ever-creative hostess, invited nearly two dozen of us over to her mother's lovely home and fed us spinach and roasted tomato strata, cinnamon coffee cake, and strong coffee. We spent the morning in vibrant community, laughing and learning, all the while doing a tiny something to help other women in our midst.

That's a good story.

My friend Angie's group of passionate, capable moms spearheaded a campaign they called "Plight of the Orphan," and raised over $50,000 for their church's orphan ministry. They've used that money to celebrate, educate, and support local families who have been impacted by foster care and adoption. They've carved out a space within their community for all types of families and have poured their hearts and resources into making sure their church is known as one of inclusion, social action, and compassion. It's something that Angie and her friends think about and pray about every single day.

Theirs is another good story of lives well lived.

Maybe you've heard of the group of mothers in Tennessee who, for thirty-five years, have been secretly doing good for the brokenhearted and underresourced members of their community. Inspired by the generosity and the reliance on community of their grandparents' era, they began making changes in their lives—cutting coupons and doing their own laundry—so that they could reallocate their resources and give more away. For years, "the 9 Nanas" have gotten up at 4 A.M. to make hundreds of pound cakes before beginning their day. For decades, they've delivered these pound cakes anonymously, along with things like groceries and notices of utility bills paid in full. The group keeps their ears to the ground and finds out who has need. Then they jump to action by delivering a package filled with tangible items of help and nourishment with a note that says, "Somebody loves you."

In an interview with the *Huffington Post*, one of the members said this of their operation:

> We gave new meaning to the term drive-by. We'd drive through low-income neighborhoods and look for homes that had fans in the window. That told us that the people who lived there didn't have air-conditioning. Or we'd see that there were no lights on at night, which meant there was a good chance their utilities had been turned off. Then we'd return before the sun came up, like cat burglars, and drop off a little care package.[10]

For thirty-five years, this group of women (who now range in age from fifty-four to seventy-two) has been living in joyful community with one another and estimate that they've given nearly $900,000 dollars away to members of their community that they sensed could use a little help.

Another great story about love in action.

So many of us were haunted by photographer Nilüfer Demir's photo of the three-year-old Syrian boy named Alan Kurdi lying facedown on a Turkish beach after he drowned, along with his brother and their mother, trying to escape to Europe. The photo went viral on social media in September 2015 and shook much of the Western world awake to the refugee crisis happening in our midst.[11] Among those outraged was Cristal Logothetis, a mom from California who responded by starting an Indiegogo crowdfunding campaign to raise money to purchase and deliver baby carriers, slings, and wraps to Syrian refugees, believing the gesture would provide security and relief for moms and dads making the arduous journey to a better life in asylum destinations. What began as a modest goal of 100 carriers / $2,500 has since become a registered nonprofit that has raised nearly $200,000 and delivered and fitted thousands upon thousands of baby carriers to refugees in a humanitarian crisis that is very much still taking place.[12]

Yet another example of love in action.

Emily threw a birthday party at a local brewery to raise money for economic development activities for farmers living in rural, sub-Saharan Africa. Shayna creates intricate spreadsheets that help organize a massive fundraising event each year. Mary gives away countless hours of her design skill to her favorite nonprofits. Jen and her son Isaac planned and hosted a lemonade stand in their front yard on a sunny summer afternoon to support UNICEF.

The stories of love in action pile up each and every day.

These stories belong to YOU.

I pray that, like these groups and individuals, the character in the story of my life will have done the deep contemplative practice necessary to awaken her consciousness. That she'll take the long view and recognize that her actions matter. She'll seize the reigns of the story and, even though it's hard or seemingly impossible, she'll wrestle her resources, gather her girlfriends, harness her inner strength, and give Mama Bear a starring role. The action will undoubtedly rise and fall, but all the while, she'll proceed down the long road with examined courage, love, care, and compassion. I pray that over and over again, I am obedient to God and I choose the road toward love.

I hope all of us become part of a story that centers on friendship and growth and action. I hope that we all spend our resources while we're alive and leave nothing but a wake of stubborn love behind. I hope we can all find and fit into a community of women who work together to push love, joy, and compassion into the world. I hope we all learn to respond to the beams of God's love with passion and the reckless expenditure of goodness. I hope that when we gather as women, we have the courage to bring our true selves to the table and that we support one another, learn from one another, and make powerful gestures toward good. At the end of the day, I hope that all of us are bone-tired in the best possible way—blessed are the days when we go to bed exhausted because we're loving our family, our friends, and our world so well. I hope we usher in a Mama Bear revolution in which more and more mothers and women make a daily practice of giving love away near and far and with the strength, mercy, courage, and power they hold inside.

Becoming a mother is a profound gift and an unbelievable challenge. The incredible adventure is a ripe opportunity to grow and love in friendship and in relationship with God. This deep rumble is my prayer for you.

> *May motherhood awaken a beautiful new light inside of you and may you embrace the challenges and the joys of caring for and cherishing another life with the very deepest, most raw sense of your being.*
>
> *May you journey down the road of motherhood and life with a group of women to laugh with, eat with, stroll with, and share the joy, stress, and holy responsibility of raising children with. May you love and serve one another and come to understand that life is better—more joyful and more meaningful—because you do.*

May you put in the hard work of building authentic relationships and then reap the amazing benefits of these prayerfully cultivated female friendships, remembering that when your sister is cared for and celebrated, we're all cared for and celebrated, and that love and goodness are infinite.

May you help one another identify your anger and may you celebrate your passion and God-given talents. Together, may you listen to your righteous anger, recognize your privilege, and lend it to others. May you train Mama Bear and use her incredible power to ease someone else's suffering.

May you groom your group of Mama Bears and unlock every last ounce of their strength and beauty. May you channel that power and use it for good. And in doing so, may your group of Mama Bears—strong, courageous, determined Mama Bears—wreak beautiful havoc on this world.

NOTES

[1] Rose Mary Dougherty, *Group Spiritual Direction: Community for Discernment,* (New York: Paulist Press, 1995), 25.

[2] Ibid., 33—emphasis mine.

[3] I love the mystic poet Rumi's description: "Chew quietly your sweet sugarcane God-Love, and stay playfully childish." *The Essential Rumi* (San Francisco: HarperCollins, 1995), 46.

[4] Just like Andrew and his brothers as Jesus invited them to drop their nets and follow his revolution. (Matt. 4:18–20)

[5]From "The Little Black Boy," a poem by William Blake, in *Songs of Innocence and Experience*. The whole line reads: "And we are put on earth a little space, That we may learn to bear the beams of love."

[6]Henri J. M. Nouwen, *Bread for the Journey: A Daybook of Wisdom and Faith* (New York: HarperOne, 2006), "Doing Love: June 16."

[7]"Child Hunger Facts," Feeding America, accessed July 25, 2016, http://www .feedingamerica.org/hunger-in-america/impact-of-hunger/child-hunger /child-hunger-fact-sheet.html.

[8]Joan Halifax, "Compassion's Edge States and Caring Better," *On Being* podcast, December 26, 2013, http://www.onbeing.org/program/compassions -edge-states/4980.

[9]Donald Miller, "What If Your Life Could Be More Engaging Than Television?" *Storyline* blog, accessed July 22, 2016, http://storylineblog.com /2012/04/24/using-story-as-a-guide/.

[10]Lori Weiss, "It Ain't Over: The Business 9 Women Kept a Secret for Three Decades," *Huffington Post*, June 20, 2012, accessed July 16, 2016, http://www .huffingtonpost.com/2012/06/20/it-aint-over-the-business-secret_n_1607385.html.

[11]The photo was shared by Peter Bouckaert of Human Rights Watch on social media in 2015.

[12]Kimberly Yam, "Syrian Refugees Need Baby Carriers to Safely Transport Kids. Here's How to Help," *Huffington Post,* September 30, 2015, accessed July 25, 2016, http://www.huffingtonpost.com/entry/baby-carriers-syria-refugees _us_560aa58ee4b0dd8503092749. Support her Indiegogo campaign here: https:// www.indiegogo.com/projects/carry-the-future-s-baby-carriers-for-refugees#/.

FURTHER
RESOURCES

Fuel for Your Fire

To be wise is to be eternally curious.
—**Frederick Buechner**

The moment is now. As you find yourselves inspired and ready to leap, your group may enjoy reading and discussing the following books together as a group. Each book will prompt important conversation, help spark an ongoing journey, and provide wisdom along the way. As you discuss, be mindful that you won't always agree with one another. These are meant to start conversations, not necessarily form final consensus.

As you work to be the change that you want to see in this world, your moms' group will come up with your own unique ways to share your abundant love. Following the book recommendations is a list of reputable organizations that serve as mere suggestions of places that might align with your passion and your plan. Of course, your local community will have unique organizations and causes that you can pour your collective passion into and, with a little creativity, you'll find exactly the right fit. Just don't wait to take the plunge. Mama Bear is primed and ready. It's time to set her free.

BOOKS TO DEVOUR

Half the Sky: Turning Oppression into Opportunity for Women Worldwide by Nicholas D. Kristof and Sheryl WuDunn—This provocative, persuasive, and passionate book should be at the top of your list as your group gets serious about opening your eyes to the world around you. The content is an astonishing reality check for those of us living comfortable lives here in the United States. You'll feel both heartbroken and inspired as you turn each page of this fiercely pivotal book. Although you'll want to cover your eyes during some of the difficult stories presented by these two deeply caring Pulitzer-Prize winners, it's imperative that you don't. What you'll take away is a deep ache for the world as well as a newfound courage and passion to make a difference. This is a must-read for your moms' group, your mothers, your partners, your friends, and, someday, your children.

A Path Appears: Transforming Lives, Creating Opportunity by Nicholas D. Kristof and Sheryl WuDunn—A follow-up to their first book, *Half the Sky*, Kristof and WuDunn offer a narrative about making a difference both at home and abroad. As noted in Chapter Four, I had the chance to ask WuDunn what I could do to make change in the world at a lecture she gave focusing on women and social justice. Her answer? Figure out what you're passionate about and get together with your friends. "It's more fun that way," she said. On a larger scale, *A Path Appears* is an answer to my question. The book educates and inspires.

The Irresistible Revolution: Living as an Ordinary Radical by Shane Claiborne—This book is a tremendous eye-opener that will be sure to spark fantastic conversation within your moms' group. You may not all agree with some of Claiborne's assertions and actions, but you will most certainly learn from his unique perspective and animated style. If nothing else, because Claiborne believes that "we can do more together than we can do alone," your moms' group will come to value the wisdom he presents in this book, which will dare you page after page to spring into action.

Nice Girls Don't Change the World by Lynne Hybels—In this book, Lynne Hybels tells the story of her transformation from a shy, quiet mother of two to a fierce speaker, author, and activist who conquered her insecurities and fears and has since worked to bring thoughtful change to the world. A small book that your moms' group could read in a week, Hybels's words will inspire you to share your own struggles with one another and prompt you to banish whatever may be holding you back from rocking the world around you.

The Missional Mom: Living with Purpose at Home and in the World by Helen Lee—Helen Lee's well-researched book is for the mother who wants to live her life out loud. She offers great examples of phenomenal women who are professionalizing motherhood and giving back to the world in amazing and sometimes unconventional ways. Her references to Scripture are abundant and her voice is sisterly. Your moms' group would do well to read and discuss this book with one another. The content will give you further confidence in your unique journey. The book includes accountability questions that will stir discussion.

Seven by Jen Hatmaker—This book will challenge you to think deeply about the way in which you are living out your faith. Hatmaker urgently questions the middle- to upper-class American lifestyle and encourages readers to examine their everyday habits. The pages are full of energy and her message is at times convicting. Hatmaker reiterates the all-encompassing love of God, while simultaneously calling us to action in authentic ways.

One Thousand Gifts by Ann Voskamp—Reading Voskamp's book will encourage you to slow down and be thankful for every day. Sometimes as you prepare yourself for battle, it's easy to get caught up in all of the pain and suffering in the world. Voskamp doesn't ignore the struggles, but she helps readers see that by embracing the beauty in the ordinary, we will be better prepared to be fierce advocates of love and beauty. Her poetic prose and constant discipline will inspire your group to take a look at the community in which you live and prompt you to use your unique place in life to become a more active member in the lives of those around you.

The Power of Asset Mapping by Luther Snow—As you get down to the nuts and bolts of the work that your moms' group does, asset mapping will serve as an effective organizational tool. Asset mapping is an approach to coming up with solutions and carrying out missions within a community that relies on categorizing the strengths and capacities of involved individuals. Snow is a community developer who writes about leadership and organization in a way that can be applied to the mission of your group. The book is instructional, particularly for congregations who are bent on action, and will be an informative read for your missional moms' group.

Overdressed: The Shockingly High Cost of Cheap Fashion by Elizabeth Cline—This fascinating book looks at the nature of the way we buy and use clothes in America and examines the effects of our buying habits on the environment and the rest of the world. Cline shows how we can use our dollars to create change and break the buy-and-toss cycle by supporting stylish sustainable designers and retailers, returning to custom clothing, refashioning clothes throughout their lifetime, and mending and even making the clothes themselves. The history and reportage Cline provides is utterly fantastic. This book will prompt much thought and interesting conversation.

The Bible—It should go without saying that before you enter the battle, you need to be grounded with a plan. Studying the Bible with your moms' group is a great way to be held accountable for keeping your nose in Scripture. Countless studies are available to help guide you. By collectively completing Bible studies and reading the Bible, you will learn about God, and through your group discussion, you'll also learn from and about one another. Don't be intimidated. When you engage in Bible study, relationships will be strengthened and so will your knowledge of our Maker.

ORGANIZATIONS TO EXPLORE

The Adventure Project
theadventureproject.org

Remember Jody Landers, the woman who spearheaded the phenomenal Water for Christmas movement in Chapter Eleven and wrote the Foreword to this book? She eventually moved to Washington with her family and cofounded a nonprofit organization called The Adventure Project (TAP) with another phenomenal woman named Becky Straw. The Adventure Project invests in entrepreneurs in developing countries, rallying behind individuals in an effort to alleviate extreme poverty and create jobs. In just a few years, through social enterprise, the tribe has provided charcoal-efficient stoves to families in Haiti and irrigation pumps in Kenya, as well as trained mobile well mechanics in India and health-care professionals in Uganda. Jody still believes in channeling the power of motherhood, and many of the projects TAP takes on can only be done with the support of the moms in your posse. With the purchase of this book, you've already begun supporting this organization—10 percent of what you spent on this book goes to TAP!

Empower Tanzania

www.empowertz.org

Empower Tanzania is a small NGO that works in partnership with the people of rural Tanzania, providing economic empowerment, integrated farming, and educational support to vulnerable children. Since Empower Tanzania was established in 2008, thousands of rural Tanzanians have experienced improved health care, education, and economic opportunity through its model of development and sustainability. Their most dominant governing principal is to listen, listen again, and listen once more before making a suggestion. The organization believes that this posture of growth paired with their ability to strengthen and support is what makes their mission efficient and their work sustainable. Full disclosure: I contract with Empower Tanzania to handle their communications and development. I have traveled with the organization to Tanzania twice and I correspond with Tanzanian colleagues daily. I have seen the work of this organization firsthand, and it has gained my full trust, confidence, and enthusiasm.

charity: water

charitywater.org

Based in New York, charity: water is a highly recognized organization that has raised millions of dollars, changing the lives of hundreds of thousands of people by providing clean and fresh water solutions in places that are without. Charity: water, which is mentioned in this book's Foreword, takes 100 percent of all donations directly to water solution projects and follows up with proof—pictures and Google Earth coordinates of all completed projects. Unclean water is the leading cause of death in undeveloped nations, and unsanitary water kills 45,000 people each week, 90 percent of them children under the age of five. Charity: water is quickly and effectively providing solutions to this global crisis and encouraging others to join the march. The organization's use of technology and social media and their embrace of creativity make it easy for individuals to come together to build their own well and ease the suffering of many.

UNICEF
unicef.org

The United Nations Children's Emergency Fund is a worldwide organization specializing in the care and advocacy of children. It focuses on child protection, survival and development, education and gender equality, HIV/AIDS education and care, and policy advocacy. UNICEF is well established in the area of emergency relief for countries in crisis. Because their highest concern regards the good of children, this respected organization will likely speak to you as a mother.

The ONE Campaign
one.org

You may have heard of ONE, a campaign for a better world cofounded in 2002 by Bono. With 2.5 million members, ONE is a grassroots advocacy and campaigning organization that fights extreme poverty and preventable disease, particularly in Africa, by raising public awareness and pressuring political leaders to support smart and effective policies and programs that are saving lives, helping to put kids in school, and improving futures. As a member of the ONE campaign, you'll receive frequent email updates inviting your participation in everything from helping shape policy to using your consumer power to send a message to the world.

Doctors without Borders/Médecins Sans Frontières

doctorswithoutborders.org

Doctors without Borders is an international medical humanitarian organization created by doctors and journalists who saw a need for independent, impartial assistance to people whose survival is threatened by violence, neglect, or catastrophe, primarily due to armed conflict, epidemics, malnutrition, exclusion from health care, or natural disasters. Doctors without Borders is also known to speak out to bring attention to neglected crises, challenge inadequacies or abuse of the aid system, and to advocate for improved medical treatments and protocols. Because of the life-threatening health needs throughout the world, Doctors without Borders is an integral agent in relieving suffering and offering hope to the hopeless.

The Hunger Project

thp.org

The Hunger Project is a global nonprofit whose mission is to end hunger in Africa, South Asia, and Latin America by providing sustainable solutions based on self-reliance for those most affected by hunger. Much of their work focuses on empowering women as key agents of change and ending violence and oppression against them. The Hunger Project welcomes volunteer activists to help raise money and advocate for those in dire need of assistance.

The Glass Slipper Project

glassslipperproject.org

Based in Chicago, the Glass Slipper Project helps outfit girls for prom who may not otherwise be able to afford all the fashionable trappings that help make the high school milestone memorable. This volunteer-run organization collects previously worn formal wear and accessories and invites girls to shop their well-curated selection at Glass Slipper "boutiques" throughout the city. Each young woman has the help of a volunteer personal shopper to guide her through the shopping process. Though the Glass Slipper Project is not currently a widespread operation, the website offers resources for anyone interested in engaging in a similar project in their own city or town.

YMCA and YWCA

Check out your community YMCA or YWCA for opportunities to serve your own neighborhood or city. The Y is known for its long tradition of helping community members in all sorts of endeavors—from life coaching to mentoring to practices in healthy living. The YMCA, as well as similar organizations found within your community, relies on individual volunteers to help those who are down on their luck or who need a little extra care and attention. As the health and well-being of American children is a major concern today, the YMCA may be a good fit for your talent and passion.

Local Schools, Churches, Women's Shelters, and Food Pantries

There is certainly room for ingenuity, but there is no need to reinvent the wheel. As you decide how your group is best equipped to serve, look for organizations within your community who are already doing it. Then roll up your sleeves and lend a hand. Don't forget to look in the obvious places. Chances are, you are already familiar with your local school district, have a foot in the door of your church, and know of a few pantries in your area. If not, start asking around for opportunities that might match your collective interest. Once you've found a spot to serve, get creative, whisper a prayer, and prepare to astonish the people around you with the heart, energy, and know-how of your moms' group.

A FOUR-WEEK
GROUP GUIDE

Week One

Discussion prompts in response to Part One of *Mama Bear's Manifesto*.

1. In her Introduction, the author tells us about stepping out of her comfort zone on two different occasions and joining circles of women who found themselves in similar life stages. What do you think the benefits of meeting together in community are? In your experience, how does time spent with one another help us grow as individuals and mothers? How do you feel when you approach these situations?

2. In "Meeting Mama Bear," the idea of using our innate Mama Bear passion and channeling it for good is introduced. What makes you angry? Beyond petty grievances, what makes your blood boil and your Mama Bear roar to life?

3. Throughout the first section of the book, the author gives examples of women who leverage their joy and talent to impact the world around them. What activities do you love as an individual and find to bring peace and joy to your soul? Don't be shy: What gifts has God bestowed upon you?

4. Start dreaming: How might we harness our anger as a moms' group, identify our collective interests and strengths, and work for good in the world?

Week Two

Discussion prompts in response to Part Two of *Mama Bear's Manifesto*.

1. After reading "Living and Loving Out Loud," consider the community of women with whom you are reading this book. In what tangible ways are you taking care of one another? At what other times in your life have you felt taken care of by a local community?

2. In "Protecting through Prayer," the author touches on her personal prayer life. If you're comfortable sharing, tell the group what your prayer patterns are. Are you at ease praying with and for others? What does an ideal prayer community look like to you?

3. As the author discusses the nuts and bolts of embracing a new ministry, she points out the importance of being intentional and good stewards of time, which is a precious commodity to all of us. How do you see to make the best use of your meeting time? How will you decide on the mission of the group? How do you envision preparing your group for action?

4. Think again about your God-given talents and the times at which you feel the most peace, joy, and purpose. How have these gifts been revealed to you? Describe yourself: Are you a dreamer, list-maker, taskmaster, artist, teacher, tastemaker, or communicator? Help each other unearth the very best things about yourselves each other one another to use those gifts in service of others.

Week Three

Discussion prompts in response to Part Three of *Mama Bear's Manifesto*.

1. The author presents a detailed list of outrageous traits in the chapter "Supermom Must Die" and then begins the long process of ridding herself of Supermom once and for all. Make

a list of your "supermom" characteristics. How would life be different if you shed these expectations?

2. Consider the current cultural landscape, jam-packed with images and statements of perfection, in part because of the instantaneous nature and skewed storytelling of social media. How does our culture impact your identity as a mom? How does this compare and contrast with God's plan for you as a mom?

3. After dismissing the idea of a souped-up Supermom, the author embraces a less shiny, but still brave, way of life. Does the idea of a simpler life appeal to you? In what ways have you simplified your life since becoming a mother? In what ways has it gotten more complicated?

4. Chapter Nine, "Do Good," focuses on perfectionism. What do you foresee as being the pitfalls of perfectionism, and how might this idea paralyze the efforts of your group? How do you move past this? How might you support one another in doing so?

Week Four

Discussion prompts in response to Part Four of *Mama Bear's Manifesto*.

1. After reading Chapter Ten, how might your group prepare yourselves for conflict? In what ways will you work to resolve any conflict that may arise within your group as you endeavor to harness the energy and power of motherhood and do good in the world?

2. What part of the Water for Christmas story appeals to you most? If such an effort had taken root in your community, where do you envision yourself most joyfully taking part? Organizing a road race? Encouraging local high school students? Managing social media? How might you duplicate something of this sort within your own sphere of influence?

3. When do you most clearly hear God's voice? In what ways are you able to discern whether or not you are following his plan for your life?

4. After reading *Mama Bear's Manifesto*, do you feel inspired to seize your anger, mobilize your talent, and serve the world around you? After careful consideration, is this right for your group at this time? What might this look like at this moment in time?

Acknowledgments

Years ago, I was struck by an idea Gary Wills presented in his book *What Jesus Meant*: writing about God and what's holy should be done on your knees. It is from this metaphorical posture of worship that I attempted to make *Mama Bear's Manifesto* flow. I thank God (Love-with-a-Capital-L) for this life, these words, and for constantly showing himself in the people that I love.

I am profoundly grateful to my Chicago moms' group. Holly, Jen, Lindsay, Vicky, Lisa, Tasha, Melissa, Kara, Sarah, Veronica—we adventured through the dazzling and terrifically challenging early years of motherhood together and you will forever be a very large part of my beating heart. You changed me in incredible ways and I am thankful for your sweet, unwavering friendship and care. The moments we shared studying, discussing, and pushing strollers down city streets were both magical and transformative.

To the tribe of women in my community that blesses my life daily—Emily, Beth, Sara, Amy, Lisa—thank you for sharing your laughter, advice, encouragement, coffee, and wine. Thank you for showing up over and over again and for inspiring me constantly with the way you walk through this world with such strength, tenderness, intelligence, and absolute magnificence. For someone who did not grow up with sisters, I have found so many! I constantly stand in awe of all of the good women that I've gotten to know in this life—those mentioned in this book and beyond. I have landed in a community full of movers and shakers and the most beautiful hearts and capable hands. Look around! Good people are everywhere!

Many thanks to my sister-in-law, Tesi, for always laughing at my jokes and for the nonstop encouragement, wisdom, and love. I can't imagine a life without you—you have been my constant co-conspirator (check out our podcast: Mama Bear Dares!) since we married a pair of brothers all those years ago. I knew that when I married Jake good things were in store—I had no idea I'd end up sharing a last name with so many luminous, passionate souls!

I'm eternally thankful to Becky for her friendship, all of her writer-ly encouragement, and for sharing so many mornings of writing and editing while our children played underfoot. Thanks to Clark for always engaging in lively, fascinating discussion and for the careful reading of the early drafts of this book. The two of you, along with Cynthia, provided the encouragement, wisdom, and critical eye that only the most honest and generous writers' group could. I'm forever grateful! Thanks also to my agent, Chip MacGregor, for believing in the idea that moms can change the world, and to Mary Hardegree, the managing editor at Leafwood Publishers, for making the process of bringing this book into the world so delightful.

My mother, to whom this book is dedicated, exemplifies the most tender and fierce of all Mama Bears. For over three decades she has shown me a thoughtful, informed, outrageous, and outward love rooted in a deep sense of justice. Her love and example are everything to me.

Motherhood has brought my greatest joy and biggest challenge. My heart bursts day after day with love and gratitude for the children who call me mom: Oliver, Elihu, and Sintayehu. Thank you, dear children, for awakening my Mama Bear and for being so sweet, hilarious, and beautifully complicated. The three of you are my greatest joys.

And finally, thank you to Jake, my great love. Thank you for believing in me, for always giving me not only the green light but also the nudge I need to pursue my crazy ideas, for all of the life-giving kitchen and car conversations, and for your steadfast love and constant hilarity. You continually challenge me to live boldly and love better. And for all the Saturday mornings that I would have rather remained sitting on the couch, thank you for pushing me out the door to the coffee shop so that I could finish this book. You are my everything.